The Obamacare Hypocrites

341 reasons why Democrats and unions that support Obamacare want exemptions for themselves

By Daniel Alman

Note: The print version of this book is a companion to the Amazon Kindle version. Only the Kindle version includes citations to references and sources. The print version does not include these citations. All of the citations in the Kindle version are internet links to online sources. Every claim that I make in this book is sourced in the Kindle version. Click on the underlined text (only in the Kindle version) to see the sources.

Since there are quite a few people named Daniel Alman in the world, it is worth noting that this particular Daniel Alman was born in 1971, and has spent his entire life so far living in the Squirrel Hill neighborhood of Pittsburgh, Pennsylvania. He has a bachelor's degree in mathematics from the University of Pittsburgh, but even more importantly (at least in his opinion), he attended the Montessori Centre Academy in Glenshaw, Pennsylvania, for ten years, beginning at the age of two. His blog is at https://danfromsquirrelhill.wordpress.com/

The first print version of this book was originally published on September 29, 2018. This version was last updated on September 29, 2018.

* * * * * * *

Obamacare is so horrible that many of the Democrats and unions that helped to pass it ended up asking for exemptions for themselves.

Many of these exemptions were granted to them by President Obama, without approval from Congress, which makes these exemptions illegal.

You should never trust anyone who isn't willing to live by the same rules that they expect everyone else to live by.

This book is a comprehensive criticism of Obamacare, with many of these criticisms coming from the very people who helped to get Obamacare passed in the first place.

* * * * * *

1) **After Obamcare was passed, unions that supported its passage requested and received special exemptions**

Within months after Obamacare was passed, Obama gave some organizations an exemption from some of the requirements of Obamacare. As time went on, more than 1,300 organizations received these exemptions.

More than half of the people who are covered by insurance plans that received these exemptions are in union insurance plans. These unions supported the passage of Obamacare. But immediately after Obamacare was passed, these unions wanted exemptions from the very same law that they wanted to force everyone else to obey. This reveals an extreme level of hypocrisy among many of the supporters of Obamacare.

In addition, these exemptions are illegal for two reasons - because Obama granted the exemptions without approval from Congress, and because the Constitution requires the law to treat everyone the same.

The Washington Times <u>wrote</u> of this:

"Selective enforcement of the law is the first sign of tyranny. A government empowered to determine arbitrarily who may operate outside the rule of law invariably embraces favoritism as friends, allies and those with the best-funded lobbyists are rewarded. Favoritism inevitably leads to corruption, and corruption invites extortion. Ultimately, the rule of law ceases to exist in any recognizable form, and what is left is tyranny."

"The now-familiar monthly trickling down of new waivers is, at best, a tacit admission that Obamacare is a failure. So far, seven entire states and 1,372 businesses, unions and other institutions have received waivers from the law. The list includes the administration's friends and allies and, of course, those who have the best lobbyists."

"More than 50 percent of the Obamacare waiver beneficiaries are union members, which is striking because union members account for less than 12 percent of the American work force. The same unions that provided more than $120 million to Democrats in the last two elections and, in many cases, openly campaigned in favor of the government takeover of your health care, now celebrate that Obamacare is not their problem."

2) After Obamacare was passed, politicians who voted for it asked for a special exemption for their own districts

Even the politicians who voted for Obamacare want exemptions for their own districts.

In response to the medical device tax that is part of Obamacare, some medical device manufacturers have announced plans to layoff employees, including Welch Allyn (275 planned layoffs), Stryker (1,170 planned layoffs), and Medtronic (1,000 planned layoffs).

In December 2012, Al Franken, Elizabeth Warren, John Kerry, and 15 other Democrats who supported the passage of Obamacare wrote a letter to Harry Reid, asking him to delay the tax on medical devices, claiming that the tax would hurt job creation in their districts.

3) Politicians who voted for Obamacare wanted an additional exemption for themselves and their staff after it was passed

This is another example of how the politicians who voted for Obamacare want exemptions for themselves.

In 2010, Obamacare was passed by the House and Senate, and signed by President Obama.

Three years later, members of Congress and their staff complained that Obamacare was going to cost them a lot of money, and said that this would likely cause a brain drain among their staff. In response to this, Obama made changes to Obamacare so that these things would not happen. However, Obama's actions were illegal, because he made these changes without Congress voting on them first.

The New York Times wrote of this:

> *... the language of the health care law requires Congressional employees to obtain health insurance through an exchange created by the law, but other parts of the federal legal code restrict the ability of the federal government to pay the usual employer share for group insurance programs approved by the Office of Personnel Management.*

> *A straightforward reading of the law thus means that Congressional staff members, starting in January 2014, will have to obtain insurance through the Affordable Care Act but pay for it on their own without the normal contribution from their employer — Congress. This would be a multi-thousand-dollar income hit for those affected... many... would potentially feel the pain, giving rise to concerns over a potential brain drain of Congressional staff members finding other employment.*

> *... the federal personnel office initially ruled that Congressional staff members would not be eligible for the subsidies, and then changed this decision under pressure from the White House...*

4) An entire state that supported Obamacare asked for an exemption

The people of Massachusetts were huge supporters of Obamacare when it was passed, and they voted for Obama in both elections. But even they eventually ended up asking for their own special exemption from Obamacare.

In August 2013, Obama gave an Obamacare waiver to Massachusetts.

This waiver was illegal for two reasons. First, the waiver was not approved by the U.S. Congress. Second, the U.S. Constitution requires that the federal government treat all states the same.

5) Obamacare supporters at Democratic Underground later complained about it

For some really hilarious displays of shock and outrage by supporters of Obamacare at how it's harming people, check out these threads at Democratic Underground: one, two, three, four, five, six, and seven.

6) Union members quit their union because of Obamacare

The AFL-CIO was a big supporter of the passaage of Obamacare in 2010, and supported Obama in both elections.

In September 2013, it was reported that 40,000 longshoremen had quit the AFL-CIO, and that they had cited Obamacare as one of their reasons for doing so.

7) Obama broke his own deadline for creating healthcare exchanges

Even Obama himself seems to be an opponent of Obamacare.

Three years after Obama signed Obamacare, the New York Times reported that Obama would miss his own deadline for creating some of the insurance exchanges for small businesses.

8) Obama waited until after the 2012 election to release

unpopular Obamacare rules

Obama himself is so much against Obamacare that he waited until after the 2012 election to release some of its rules.

In April 2013, the New York Times reported:

... even fervent supporters of the law admit that things are going worse than expected.

... the Obama administration didn't want to release unpopular rules before the election.

Everything is turning out to be more complicated than originally envisioned.

A law that was very confusing has become mind-boggling... Americans are just going to be overwhelmed and befuddled. Many are just going to stay away, even if they are eligible for benefits.

9) Obama illegally bypassed Congress to delay Obamacare's employer mandate

Here's another example of how even Obama is against Obamacare.

As the Obamacare law was written, the employer mandate was to begin in January 2014. This is what the law said when it was passed by the House and Senate, and signed by President Obama in 2010.

However, in July 2013, Obama <u>delayed</u> the employer mandate part of Obamacare until January 2015. Obama did this without approval from Congress.

For Obama to change a law that was passed by Congress, without first getting approval from Congress, is a violation of the Presidential oath that Obama took to uphold and defend the Constitution.

What Obama did here is an action of a dictator, not an action of a President whose power is limited by a written constitution.

If Obama can get away with this, then it sets a horribly dangerous precedent, and means that the President can arbitrarily make any change to any law that has been passed by Congress, without first getting approval from Congress.

10) Obama illegally avoided enforcing the required income verification of people who receive subsidies for Obamacare exchanges

Here is yet another example of how Obama is against Obamacare.

Even though Obamacare requires the government to verify the income of people who receive subsidies for Obamacare exchanges, in August 2013 it was <u>reported</u> that Obama would not be verifying their incomes.

11) Obama illegally delayed the caps on out of pocket payments without Congressional approval

And here is yet one more example of how Obama is against

Obamacare.

As it was passed by the House and Senate and signed by Obama in 2010, Obamacare sets caps on the out of pocket payments that people pay for health care, and these caps were legally required to take effect in January 2014.

However, in August 2013, Obama delayed these caps until January 2015.

Because Obama imposed this delay without it first being approved by Congress, Obama's action was illegal. The President does not have the legal authority to change an Act that was passed by Congress, without that change first being approved by Congress. What Obama did here is not the act of a President whose power is limited by a written constitution, but is, instead, the action of a dictator.

12) Obama illegally prevented individual employees of small businesses from choosing their own plan during the first year of Obamacare

Here's another example of how Obama is against Obamacare.

Obamacare requires that individual employees of small businesses be allowed to choose their own insurance plan during the first year of Obamacare. However, in March 2013, the Obama administration announced that it would not be allowing them to make this choice during the first year.

13) Unions that supported the passage of Obamacare in 2010 wanted new special exempetions in 2013

Here's more hypocrisy from the unions that helped to get Obamacare passed.

In January 2013, the Wall Street Journal <u>reported</u>:

Some Unions Grow Wary of Health Law They Backed

Labor unions enthusiastically backed the Obama administration's health-care overhaul when it was up for debate. Now that the law is rolling out, some are turning sour.

Union leaders say many of the law's requirements will drive up the costs for their health-care plans and make unionized workers less competitive. Among other things, the law eliminates the caps on medical benefits and prescription drugs used as cost-containment measures in many health-care plans. It also allows children to stay on their parents' plans until they turn 26.

Some 20 million Americans are covered by the health-care plans at issue

Top officers at the International Brotherhood of Teamsters, the AFL-CIO and other large labor groups plan to keep pressing the Obama administration to expand the federal subsidies to these jointly run plans, warning that unionized employers may otherwise drop coverage. A handful of unions say they already have examined whether it makes sense to shift workers off their current plans

"We are going back to the administration to say that this is not acceptable," said Ken Hall, general secretary-treasurer for the Teamsters, which has 1.6 million members and dependents in

health-care plans. Other unions involved in the push include the United Food and Commercial Workers International Union and Unite Here

Sheet Metal Workers Local 85 in Atlanta, which has about 1,900 members. Next year it must lift the $250,000 annual cap on the amount it will pay for medical claims. The law's requirements will add between 50 cents to $1 an hour to the cost of members' compensation package

14) Obama lied about putting health care negotiations on C-SPAN

Although Obama had made a campaign promise to have all of the health care reform negotiations broadcast on C-SPAN, he broke that promise after he was elected.

The secrecy of these negotiations was so strong that U.S. Congresswoman and Speaker of the House Nancy Pelosi (D-California) said, "We have to pass the bill so that you can find out what is in it."

15) Obama lied about letting people keep their health insurance

Before Obamacare was passed, Obama said:

"No matter how we reform health care, we will keep this promise to the American people... If you like your health care plan, you'll be able to keep your health care plan, period. No one will take it away, no matter what."

Also before Obamacare was passed, Obama said:

"Here is a guarantee that I've made. If you have insurance that you like, then you will be able to keep that insurance."

However, after Obamacare was passed, the Congressional Budget Office said that the law would cause seven million people to lose their employer provided insurance.

After Obamacare was passed, 1199SEIU United Healthcare Workers East announced that it would drop health insurance for the children of more than 30,000 low-wage home attendants. Mitra Behroozi, executive director of benefit and pension funds for 1199SEIU stated

"... new federal health-care reform legislation requires plans with dependent coverage to expand that coverage up to age 26... meeting this new requirement would be financially impossible."

Also, after Obamacare was passed, the Franciscan University of Steubenville dropped its coverage in response to the law.

Universal Orlando dropped its coverage for part time employees in response to Obamacare.

In addition, after Obamacare was passed, Forbes reported

"The House Ways and Means Committee has released a new report that sheds light onto how Obamacare incentivizes companies to dump their workers onto the new law's subsidized exchanges."

Also after Obamacare was passed, MSN reported

"The Affordable Care Act mandate most commonly known as Obamacare has some tight stipulations that, CNN says, are forcing health care companies to rip up most of their current plans and draft new ones that comply. According to a University of Chicago study, just about half of the individual health care plans currently on the market won't cut it once key provisions of the Affordable Care Act kick in next year."

Furthermore, it was reported that Obamacare would cause 58,000 Aetna and UnitedHealth Group customers in California to lose their insurance.

In response to Obamacare, some employers have dropped coverage for their employees' spouses. In August 2013, it was reported that UPS had announced that it would be dropping 15,000 spouses of its employees from its health insurance, and that it had cited Obamacare as the reason it was doing this.

The chain of Wegmans supermarkets cancelled the policies of its part time employees in response to Obamacare.

In July 2013, leaders of the Teamsters, UFCW, and UNITE-HERE sent a letter to Harry Reid and Nancy Pelosi which said that Obamacare

"will shatter not only our hard-earned health benefits... these restrictions will make non-profit plans like ours unsustainable... we can no longer stand silent in the face of elements of the Affordable Care Act that will destroy the very health and well being of our members along with millions of other hardworking Americans"

In August 2013, it was <u>reported</u> that 106,000 New Jersey citizens would lose their health insurance because of Obamacare.

In September 2013, IBM <u>announced</u> that it would be switching 110,000 of its retirees from their current IBM-provided health insurance to the Obamacare exchanges.

In September 2013, Trader Joe's <u>announced</u> that, in response to Obamacare, it would stop providing insurance to its part time employees.

In October 2013, it was <u>reported</u> that at least 146,000 people in Michigan would be losing their insurance because of Obamacare.

In October 2013, it was <u>reported</u> that Florida Blue would be dropping 300,000 customers because of Obamacare.

In October 2013, it was <u>reported</u> that 491,977 individual insurance plans in California would be canceled because of Obamacare.

In October 2013, it was <u>reported</u> that, in response to Obamacare, Home Depot would stop providing insurance to its part time employees.

In October 2013, it was <u>reported</u> that Obamacare was forcing CareFirst BlueCross BlueShield to cancel the insurance of 76,000 people in Virginia, Maryland, and Washington, D.C., because their policies did not meet the minimum requirements of Obamacare.

In October 2013, it was <u>reported</u> that hundreds of thousands of people in Washington state would be losing their insurance because of Obamacare.

In November 2013, it was reported that nearly nearly 250,000 people in Colorado would lose their insurance because of Obamacare.

In January 2014, it was reported that, in response to Obamacare, Target was planning to stop offering insurance to its part time employees.

16) **Obama lied about the cost of Obamacare**

Before Obamacare was passed, Obama promised

"I will not sign a plan that adds one dime to our deficits - either now or in the future. I will not sign it if it adds one dime to the deficit, now or in the future, period. And to prove that I'm serious, there will be a provision in this plan that requires us to come forward with more spending cuts if the savings we promised don't materialize."

However, after Obama signed it, the Washington Post reported that it would add more than $340 billion to the budget deficit over the next decade.

In March 2012, the Congressional Budget Office said that over the next decade, Obamacare would cost twice as much as what Obama had promised.

In May 2013, it was reported that Obamacare's program for high risk patients was more expensive than what Obama had promised.

17) Obama falsely claimed that the U.S. Supreme Court had never overturned any laws that had been passed by Congress

Despite having taught constitutional law at one of the most prestigious law schools in the country, in April 2012 Obama falsely claimed that the U.S. Supreme Court had never overturned any laws that had been passed by Congress.

18) Obama said the health insurance mandate was not a tax, but later told the Supreme Court that it was

Before Obama's health care reform was passed, he said that the mandate was not a tax. However, after it was passed, the Obama administration argued in front of the Supreme Court that the mandate really was a tax.

19) Obamacare punishes hospitals for saving the lives of patients with heart disease

Obama's health care reform contains a provision that reduces Medicare payments to hospitals with high 30-day readmission rates. Sunil Kripalani, MD, a professor with Vanderbilt University Medical Center, said of this, "Among patients with heart failure, hospitals that have higher readmission rates actually have lower mortality rates. So, which would we rather have — a hospital readmission or a death?"

20) Obamacare encourages employers to switch their employees from full time to part time

The New York Times reported that Obamacare

"sharply penalizes full-time employment in favor of part-time employment."

In response to the employer mandate of Obamacare, some restaurants have announced plans to switch some of their employees from full time to part time, including some franchises of <u>Olive Garden</u>, <u>Red Lobster</u>, <u>Wendy's</u>, <u>Taco Bell</u>, <u>White Castle</u>, and <u>Fatburger</u>.

Community College of Allegheny County <u>switched</u> 200 professors and 200 other employees from full time to part time in response to Obamacare. Clint Benjamin, an English professor at Community College of Allegheny County, <u>said</u> that this would reduce his own monthly pay by $600.

Also in response to the employer mandate of Obamacare, other colleges have <u>announced</u> plans to switch some of their employees from full time to part time, including Florida's Palm Beach State College, Ohio's Youngstown State University, and New Jersey's Kean University.

In Virginia, thousands of government employees had their hours <u>reduced</u> because of Obamacare.

The Carnegie Museum of Pittsburgh <u>reduced</u> the hours of 48 of its employees in response to Obamacare.

Regal Entertainment Group, the largest chain of movie theaters in the country, <u>announced</u> that it would be switching thousands of its employees from full time to part time in response to the Obamacare mandate.

Utah's Granite School District <u>reduced</u> the hours of 1,200 of its employees in response to Obamacare.

In response to Obamacare, many Wal-Mart stores have <u>stopped</u> hiring full time workers.

In July 2013, leaders of the Teamsters, UFCW, and UNITE-HERE sent a <u>letter</u> to Harry Reid and Nancy Pelosi which said that Obamacare will

"destroy the foundation of the 40 hour work week that is the backbone of the American middle class... the law creates an incentive for employers to keep employees' work hours below 30 hours a week. Numerous employers have begun to cut workers' hours to avoid this obligation."

In response to Obamacare, Forever 21 <u>reduced</u> its employees' hours.

As of September 2013, more than 200 public-sector employers had <u>reduced</u> their employees' hours in response to Obamacare.

Sea World <u>reduced</u> the weekly hours of its part time employees from 32 to 28 in response to Obamacare.

Lands' End <u>limited</u> its part time employees to 29 hours per week in response to Obamacare.

As of September 2013, at least 34 universities and colleges had <u>reduced</u> some of their employees' hours in response to Obamacare.

On October 23, 2013, Investor's Business Daily wrote:

IBD has a running list that now includes 351 employers that have opted to cut work hours below 30 per week or take related steps to limit liability under ObamaCare's employer mandate. Each entry is documented with links to news sources and public records.

About 275 entries on IBD's list come from the public sector, including more than 100 school districts.

21) Obama falsely said that switching to electronic medical records would make health care cheaper

Although Obama claimed that switching to electronic record keeping as part of Obamacare would make health care cheaper, it actually made it more expensive.

22) Obama falsely said that surgeons get paid between $30,000 and $50,000 for amputating a leg

In August 2009, while trying to justify the passage of Obamacare, Obama stated

"Let's take the example of something like diabetes, one of --- a disease that's skyrocketing, partly because of obesity, partly because it's not treated as effectively as it could be. Right now if we paid a family -- if a family care physician works with his or her patient to help them lose weight, modify diet, monitors whether they're taking their medications in a timely fashion, they might get reimbursed a pittance. But if that same diabetic ends up getting their foot amputated, that's $30,000, $40,000, $50,000 --

immediately the surgeon is reimbursed. Well, why not make sure that we're also reimbursing the care that prevents the amputation, right? That will save us money."

The American College of Surgeons responded to this by <u>saying</u>

"President Obama got his facts completely wrong. He stated that a surgeon gets paid $50,000 for a leg amputation when, in fact, Medicare pays a surgeon between $740 and $1,140 for a leg amputation. This payment also includes the evaluation of the patient on the day of the operation plus patient follow-up care that is provided for 90 days after the operation. Private insurers pay some variation of the Medicare reimbursement for this service."

23) Obama falsely said that doctors perform unnecessary tonsillectomies to make more money
In July 2009, Obama <u>said</u>

"Right now, doctors, a lot of times, are forced to make decisions based on the fee payment schedule that's out there. So if ... your child has a bad sore throat, or has repeated sore throats, the doctor may look at the reimbursement system and say to himself, 'You know what? I make a lot more money if I take this kid's tonsils out.'"

"Now, that may be the right thing to do. But I'd rather have that doctor making those decisions just based on whether you really need your kid's tonsils out or whether it might make more sense just to change -- maybe they have allergies. Maybe they have something else that would make a difference."

The American Academy of Otolaryngology - Head and Neck

Surgery responded by <u>saying</u>

"The AAO-HNS is disappointed by the President's portrayal of the decision making processes by the physicians who perform these surgeries. In many cases, tonsillectomy may be a more effective treatment, and less costly, than prolonged or repeated treatments for an infected throat."

24) Obama illegally added 20,000 extra pages to Obamacare without Congressional approval

After Obamacare was passed, Obama added <u>20,000 extra pages</u> to it, even though those extra 20,000 pages had not been voted on by Congress.

25) Obamacare's own authors admitted that it was a "huge train wreck" that was "beyond comprehension"

U.S. Senator Max Baucus (D-Montana), one of the authors of Obamacare, <u>said</u> of it, "I just see a huge train wreck coming down."

U.S. Senator Jay Rockefeller (D-West Virginia), another author of the law, <u>said</u> it was "beyond comprehension."

26) Obama used Obamacare to illegally give the IRS additional powers without approval from Congress

In May 2013 the Washington Post <u>wrote</u>:

The law allows the Department of Health and Human Services to set up federal health exchanges in the holdout states. But the statute makes no mention of the IRS providing credits and subsidies through federal exchanges.

The IRS resolved this conundrum by denying its existence. In a May 2012 regulatory ruling, it asserted its own right to provide credits outside the state exchanges as the reasonable interpretation of an ambiguous law. But the language of the law is not ambiguous. And health scholars Jonathan Adler and Michael Cannon, in an exhaustive recent analysis, find no justification for the IRS's ruling in the legislative history of Obamacare. "The statute," they argue, "and the lack of any support for the IRS rule in the legislative record put defenders of the IRS rule in the awkward position of arguing that it was so obviously Congress' intent to offer tax credits in federal exchanges that despite a year of debate over the PPACA, it never occurred to anyone to express that intent out loud. A better explanation is that the PPACA's authors miscalculated when they assumed states would establish exchanges."

So: The IRS seized the authority to spend about $800 billion over 10 years on benefits that were not authorized by Congress. And the current IRS scandal puts this decision in a new light. What was the role of politics in shaping this regulatory decision? What pressure was applied?

27) The Obama administration illegally solicited donations from health insurers

In May 2013, Health and Human Services Secretary Kathleen Sebelius <u>solicited</u> donations from health insurers to help pay for Obamacare. Such soliciting is <u>illegal</u>.

28) Obamacare pressures unions to reduce the amount of health insurance coverage for their employees

Still more hypocrisy from the unions that helped to pass Obamacare.

In May 2013, the New York Times <u>reported</u>:

Say goodbye to that $500 deductible insurance plan and the $20 co-payment for a doctor's office visit. They are likely to become luxuries of the past.

Expect to have your blood pressure checked or a prescription filled at a clinic at your office, rather than by your private doctor.

Then blame the so-called Cadillac tax, which penalizes companies that offer high-end health care plans to their employees.

Although the tax does not start until 2018, employers say they have to start now to meet the deadline and they are doing whatever they can to bring down the cost of their plans. Under the law, an employer or health insurer offering a plan that costs more than $10,200 for an individual and $27,500 for a family would typically pay a 40 percent excise tax on the amount exceeding the threshold.

Tom Leibfried, a legislative director for the A.F.L.-C.I.O., one of the unions whose plans are vulnerable to the tax, says the demands that workers pay more for their care is a perennial aspect of labor negotiations. "We're very concerned about the hollowing out of benefits in general," he said. "What the excise tax will do is just fuel that."

29) **Obama betrayed the people of the city that helped him launch his political career**

As part of his effort to get Obamacare passed, Obama repeatedly promised that people could keep their current health insurance if they liked it.

More than any other city, the people of Chicago helped to get Obamacare passed. Chicago is where Obama chose to live when he first got into politics. The people there launched his political career and voted him into office.

And this is how Obama repays them. In May 2013, the Chicago Tribune reported:

Mayor Rahm Emanuel plans to start reducing health insurance coverage next year for more than 30,000 retired city workers and begin shifting them to President Barack Obama's new federal system.

The move is aimed at saving the city money

Once the phaseout is complete, those retired workers would have to pay for their own health insurance or get subsidies under the Affordable Care Act. The city-subsidized coverage is particularly important to retired workers who aren't yet eligible for Medicare

Henry Bayer, executive director of the American Federation of State, County and Municipal Employees Council 31, said the uncertainties of the Affordable Care Act and the state insurance exchanges they would create make the city's plan hard to assess.

"This uncertainty will cause anxiety and fear for tens of thousands of seniors who gave their working lives to public service — men and women whose retirement savings are already under attack in the name of 'pension reform.'" Bayer said.

30) Obamacare raised the interest rate on student loans to pay for Obamacare

Obamacare raised the interest rate on students loans from 5.3% to 6.8%. The money is used to fund Obamacare.

31) Obama refused to fire or prosecute 15 IRS agents who illegally seized the medical records of 10 million people

In March 2011, 15 IRS agents illegally seized the medical records of 10 million people without a warrant. Obama refused to fire or prosecute them.

32) Obama hired 16,500 new IRS agents to run Obamacare

In June 2013, it was reported that Obama had hired 16,500 new IRS agents to run Obamacare.

33) Obamacare makes it too hard for some doctors to continue their practices

In July 2013, ABC News reported that some doctors were shutting down their practices in response to Obamacare.

Dr. Robert WcWilliams, an obstetrician/gynecologist with more than 5,000 patients, said:

"It's going to be run by bureaucrats - and it's going to be run by politicians - who have no idea what is in your best interests, then I'm getting out."

34) Obama falsely guaranteed that people could keep their doctor

Before Obamacare was passed, Obama said:

"Here is a guarantee that I've made... If you've got a doctor that you like, you will be able to keep your doctor."

However, in July 2013, the Obama administration said that people "may" be able to keep their doctor.

35) Obama broke his promise to have real time verifiability of Obamacare subsidies

In July 2013, Investor's Business Daily wrote:

Meanwhile, the administration tacitly admitted last week that its promise of real-time verification of a consumer's eligibility to buy subsidized coverage at an ObamaCare exchange wasn't exactly panning out.

Under ObamaCare, only those who don't have access to "affordable" insurance at work can buy coverage in an exchange, and only those below certain income levels are eligible for tax subsidies.

Rather than a high-tech instant check, the administration told states they could simply take the applicants' word for it when it comes to their employer-provided coverage, as well as their "projected annual household income," without the need for "further verification."

36) **Obamacare contradicts itself**

Obamacare allows insurance companies to charge higher premiums for smokers. At the same time, it prohibits insurance companies from charging more than three times as much for older people as it does for younger people. In June 2013, Obama's computer programmers said that they had been unable to write a computer program that simultaneously agreed with both of these rules.

37) **Obamacare is so horrible that even the IRS agents who run it don't want to participate in it**

Obama hired 16,500 new IRS agents to run Obamacare.

But Obamacare is so awful that even the IRS agents who run it don't want to participate in it.

In July 2013, the National Treasury Employees Union, which represents the IRS employees who will be running Obamacare, provided a form letter to its members to send to their Congressmen. The letter stated:

"I am very concerned about legislation that has been introduced

by Congressman Dave Camp to push federal employees out of the Federal Employees Health Benefits Program and into the insurance exchanges established under the Affordable Care Act."

When asked about this, IRS chief Daniel Werfel responded by saying:

"I don't want to speak for the NTEU, but I'll offer a perspective as a federal employee myself and a federal employee at the IRS. And that is, we have right now as employees of the government, of the IRS, affordable health care coverage. I think the ACA was designed to provide an option or an alternative for individuals that do not. And all else being equal, I think if you're an individual who is satisfied with your health care coverage, you're probably in a better position to stick with that coverage than go through the change of moving into a different environment and going through that process. So I think for a federal employee, I think more likely, and I would -- can speak for myself, I would prefer to stay with the current policy that I'm pleased with rather than go through a change if I don't need to go through that change."

38) **Obama falsely said that Obamacare had not hurt jobs**

In July 2013, the Obama administration said that Obamacare had not hurt jobs.

However, in the real world, in response to the medical device tax that is part of Obamacare, some medical device manufacturers have announced plans to layoff employees, including Welch Allyn (275 planned layoffs), Stryker (1,170 planned layoffs), and Medtronic (1,000 planned layoffs). In December 2012, Al Franken, Elizabeth Warren, John Kerry, and 15 other Democrats who supported the passage of Obamacare wrote a letter to Harry Reid, asking him to delay the tax on medical devices, claiming that the tax would hurt job creation in their districts. The New York Times reported that Obamacare "sharply penalizes full-time employment in favor of part-time employment." In response to the employer mandate of Obamacare, some restaurants have announced plans to switch some of their employees from full time to part time, including some franchises of Olive Garden, Red Lobster, Wendy's, Taco Bell, White Castle, and Fatburger. Community College of Allegheny County switched 200 professors and 200 other employees from full time to part time in response to Obamacare. Clint Benjamin, an English professor at Community College of Allegheny County, said that this would reduce his own monthly pay by $600. Also in response to the employer mandate of Obamacare, other colleges have announced plans to switch some of their employees from full time to part time, including Florida's Palm Beach State College, Ohio's Youngstown State University, and New Jersey's Kean University. In Virginia, thousands of government employees had their hours reduced because of Obamacare. The Carnegie Museum of Pittsburgh reduced the hours of 48 of its employees in response to Obamacare. Regal Entertainment Group, the largest chain of movie theaters in the country, announced that it would be switching thousands of its employees from full time to part time in response to the Obamacare mandate. Utah's Granite School District reduced the hours of 1,200 of its employees in response to Obamacare. In response to Obamacare, many Wal-Mart stores have stopped hiring full time workers. In response to Obamacare, Forever 21 reduced its employees' hours. As of September 2013, more than 200 public-sector employers had reduced their employees' hours in response to Obamacare. Sea World reduced the weekly hours of its part time employees from 32 to 28 in response to Obamacare. Lands' End limited its part time employees to 29 hours per week in response to Obamacare. As of September 2013, at least 34 universities and colleges had reduced some of their employees' hours in response to Obamacare. In

September 2013, it was <u>reported</u> that in response to Obamacare, Indiana University would be laying off 50 of its employees and switching them to a temp agency. In July 2013, leaders of the Teamsters, UFCW, and UNITE-HERE sent a <u>letter</u> to Harry Reid and Nancy Pelosi which said that Obamacare will "destroy the foundation of the 40 hour work week that is the backbone of the American middle class... the law creates an incentive for employers to keep employees' work hours below 30 hours a week. Numerous employers have begun to cut workers' hours to avoid this obligation."

39) Obama falsely said that health insurance premiums would be reduced by $2,500 per family by the end of his first term

In February 2008, Obama <u>said</u>:

"We are going to work with you to lower your premiums by $2,500. We will not wait 20 years from now to do it, or 10 years from now to do it. We will do it by the end of my first term as president."

However, by the time his first term was over, family premiums had gotten <u>bigger</u>, not smaller. The increase was $3,065 per family.

40) Obamacare places a 40% tax on so-called "Cadillac" insurance plans

Obamacare includes a 40% tax on so-called "Cadillac" insurance plans. In August 2013, unions that supported the passage of Obamacare <u>complained</u> about this tax.

41) Obamacare makes medical care for special needs children more expensive

In August 2013, it was <u>reported</u> that Obamacare would make it more expensive for the parents of special needs children to pay for their children's medical equipment and specialized private schools that cater to their medical needs.

42) Obamacare outlawed the low-premium, high-deductible health insurance that some people prefer

Obamacare <u>bans</u> the low-premium, high-deductible health insurance that some people prefer.

43) Obamacare creates new fines for charitable hospitals that give treatment to uninsured people

In August 2013, it was <u>reported</u> that Obamacare creates new fines for charitable hospitals that give treatment to uninsured people.

44) Obama paid $67 million to so-called "volunteers"

In August 2013, it was <u>reported</u> that Obama has paid $67 million to so-called "volunteers" to teach people about Obamacare.

45) Obama illegally used Obamacare to fund pre-K education without approval from Congress

In August 2013, it was <u>reported</u> that Obama had illegally used Obamacare to fund pre-K education without approval from Congress.

46) Obamacare is so terrible that less than 3% of federal employees want to join it

In August 2013, it was reported that less than 3% of federal employees wanted to participate in Obamacare.

47) Obama avoided doing background checks on Obamacare "navigators"

In August 2013, it was reported that the Obama administration would not be doing background checks on Obamacare "navigators," despite the fact that these "navigators" would have access to people's personal, private, and financial information.

48) Obama illegally missed half of Obamacare's deadlines

In August 2013, it was reported that Obama had illegally missed 41 of Obamacare's 82 deadlines.

49) Obama tried to give illegal Obamacare subsidies to unions without Congressional approval

In August 2013, it was reported that Obama was trying to give illegal Obamacare subsidies to unions, without approval from Congress.

50) Obamacare makes it harder for writers, actors, artists, and musicians to obtain health insurance

In September 2013, the Weekly Standard reported:

*Nancy Pelosi waxed rhapsodic in 2010 as she imagined the
benefits of Obamacare: "Think of an economy where people
could be an artist or a photographer or a writer without worrying
about keeping their day job in order to have health insurance."*

*But as Obamacare begins to kick in, artists, photographers,
writers, and other members of the "creative class" who have
access to health insurance programs through numerous
professional organizations will lose that coverage.*

*Up until now professional organizations have worked with
insurance providers to craft reduced-rate plans for their
members. But thanks to the fine print in the Patient Protection
and Affordable Care Act (PPACA), on January 1, 2014, many of
these plans will fail to pass legal muster.*

*The College Art Association website posted a notice this month:
"The New York Life Insurance Company recently informed CAA
that it will no longer offer catastrophic healthcare coverage
previously available to CAA members."*

*The Entertainment Industry Group Insurance Trust (TEIGIT)
website posts the following notice: "All individual and/or Sole
Proprietor Health Insurance will terminate January 1, 2014. This
includes plans acquired as Members of our Affiliated
Associations & their groups." Those affiliated associations
include the American Federation of Television and Radio Artists,
the Dramatists Guild, the Graphic Arts Guild, NY Women in Film
and Television, and many others.*

*This will affect huge numbers of freelance artists, musicians, disc
jockeys, and so forth.*

freelance artists, designers, and musicians forced to enter the state-run exchanges are far more likely to see their rates go up

Pelosi's vision of a world full of carefree artists, musicians, and writers is a mirage and becoming fainter the closer we get to January 1.

51) **Obamacare encourages employers to use temp agencies**

In September 2013, it was reported that in response to Obamacare, Indiana University would be laying off 50 of its employees and switching them to a temp agency.

In June 2013, Time magazine wrote:

Temp Agencies Are Learning to Love the Affordable Care Act

Staffing companies like Robert Half International and On Assignment have seen their stock prices soar since President Obama's reelection in November, as the election made it nearly certain that the implementation of the law would continue as planned. "In general [Obamacare] is viewed as something that will lead to increases in the penetration rate of temporary workers," says Tobey Sommer, an analyst with SunTrust Robinson Humphrey. Firms like Robert Half International are especially well positioned to benefit from the law, Sommer says, because they specialize in small and medium-sized companies, the very sort that may be using temporary workers to help them stay below that all-important 50-worker mark.

There's also an opening for staffing companies to present themselves as experts in the labor rules of the Obamacare law, and as a resource that other businesses can turn to for help with its many rules and regulations. "The increasing burden of these regulations will cause some clients to throw up their hands and say, 'I can't deal with all of this," says Sommer. And when that happens, a full-service staffing company could be the perfect place to seek help navigating the unknown waters of Obamacare.

52) Obamacare encourages layoffs of health care workers

In September 2013, it was reported that in response to Obamacare, Emory Healthcare, which is in Georgia, would be laying off more than 100 of its employees.

In September 2013, it was reported that in response to Obamacare, the Cleveland Clinic would be laying off some of its employees.

53) Obamacare encourages insurance companies to reduce their customers' choices of doctors and hospitals

In September 2013, the Los Angeles Times reported:

The doctor can't see you now.

Consumers may hear that a lot more often after getting health insurance under President Obama's Affordable Care Act.

To hold down premiums, major insurers in California have sharply limited the number of doctors and hospitals available to patients in the state's new health insurance market opening Oct. 1.

New data reveal the extent of those cuts in California, a crucial test bed for the federal healthcare law.

These diminished medical networks are fueling growing concerns that many patients will still struggle to get care despite the nation's biggest healthcare expansion in half a century.

Consumers could see long wait times, a scarcity of specialists and loss of a longtime doctor.

In September 2013, the New York Times reported:

... under President Obama's health care law... many insurers are significantly limiting the choices of doctors and hospitals available to consumers.

From California to Illinois to New Hampshire, and in many states in between, insurers are... restricting the number of providers who will treat patients in their new health plans.

... insurers... have created smaller networks of doctors and hospitals than are typically found in commercial insurance.

Consumers should be prepared for "much tighter, narrower networks" of doctors and hospitals, said Adam M. Linker, a health policy analyst at the North Carolina Justice Center, a statewide advocacy group.

In a new study, the Health Research Institute of PricewaterhouseCoopers, the consulting company, says that "insurers passed over major medical centers" when selecting providers in California, Illinois, Indiana, Kentucky and

Tennessee, among other states.

Juan Carlos Davila, an executive vice president of Blue Shield of California, said the network for its exchange plans... did not include the five medical centers of the University of California.

Daniel R. Hawkins Jr., a senior vice president of the National Association of Community Health Centers, which represents 9,000 clinics around the country, said "... insurers have shown little interest in including us in their provider networks."

Dr. Bruce Siegel, the president of America's Essential Hospitals, formerly known as the National Association of Public Hospitals and Health Systems, said insurers were telling his members "We don't want you in our network. We are worried about having your patients, who are sick and have complicated conditions."

In New Hampshire, Anthem Blue Cross and Blue Shield, a unit of WellPoint, one of the nation's largest insurers, has touched off a furor by excluding 10 of the state's 26 hospitals from the health plans that it will sell through the insurance exchange.

54) Obamacare encourages hospitals to close

In September 2013, WCYB <u>reported</u>:

Jonesville, Va. - A local hospital is closing its doors.

Wellmont Health System is citing unprecedented changes in health care as the reason for closing Lee Regional Medical Center.

Company officials say three reasons led to the decision reimbursement cuts associated with the Affordable Care Act, extremely low community use of the hospital and a lack of consistent physician coverage.

Lee Regional will cease all operations on October 1.

55) Obamacare requires doctors to ask patients sexual questions and put their answers in an electronic database

In September 2013, it was reported that Obamacare requires doctors to ask patients personal questions about their sex lives, and to put their answers into an electronic database. Doctors who avoid doing this will be penalized.

Dr. Adam Budzikowski, a New York cardiologist, said these sex question were "insensitive, stupid and very intrusive," and that he could not think of any reason why a cardiologist would need such information.

Dr. Richard Amerling, an associate professor of medicine at Albert Einstein Medical College, said that a patient's medical record should be "a story created by you and your doctor solely for your treatment and benefit," and that Obamacare turns doctor appointments "into an interrogation, and the data will not be confidential."

The New York Civil Liberties Union said that these requirements were a violation of patients' privacy.

The Obama administration said that patients who wished to keep their information out of the electronic database should pay in cash.

56) **Obamacare websites listed wrong prices for Obamacare**

On September 20, 2013, just 10 days before the Obamacare exchanges were legally required to be ready, it was reported that they had the wrong prices.

57) **Obama made it easier for people to commit health care fraud**

In September 2013, CNBC reported:

Deep staff cuts are hitting a federal agency responsible for investigating health-care fraud just as Obamacare is due to kick in, leaving less people to investigate an ever-growing crime that costs taxpayers billions of dollars.

And in a perverse twist, the funding cuts at the Health and Human Services Department's Inspector General's Office might save money in the short term for the U.S. taxpayer. But over the long run, more money that could have been recouped from the fraud cases now going unpursued, is being left on the table, the agency said.

For every $1 spent on health-care fraud probes, nearly $8 is recouped in fines, restitution or settlements, according to HHS.

58) **Obamacare includes a so-called "family glitch"**

In September 2013, USA Today reported:

A so-called "family glitch" in the 2010 health care law threatens to cost some families thousands of dollars in health insurance costs and leave up to 500,000 children without coverage, insurance and health care analysts say.

That's unless Congress fixes the problem, which seems unlikely given the House's latest move Friday to strip funding from the law, which is also called the Affordable Care Act.

Congress defined "affordable" as 9.5% or less of an employee's household income, mostly to make sure people did not leave their workplace plans for subsidized coverage through the exchanges. But the "error" was that it only applies to the employee — and not his or her family. So, if an employer offers a woman affordable insurance, but doesn't provide it for her family, they cannot get subsidized help through the state health exchanges.

That can make a huge difference; the Kaiser Family Foundation said an average plan for an individual is about $5,600, but it goes up to $15,700 for families.

59) Obamacare makes it harder for Canadian politicians to get health care

Canada has had so-called "universal health care" for a long time.

However, when Robert Bourassa, the premier of Quebec, Canada, needed cancer treatment, he came to the United States and paid for his health care with his own money.

And when Canadian Liberal MP Belinda Stronach needed cancer treatment, she also came to the United States and paid for her health care with her own money.

And when Newfoundland and Labrador Premier Danny Williams needed heart surgery, he, too, came to the United States and paid for his health care with his own money.

Now that Obama has given the U.S. so-called "universal health care," where will Canadian politicians go when they get sick?

60) Obamacare gives married couples an annual tax of up to $11,028 for being married instead of single

In front of the U.S. Supreme Court, the Obama administration argued that Obamacare is a tax.

According to the Obamacare calulator, Obamacare places an annual tax on married couples for being married instead of single. The amount of this tax depends upon the ages, incomes, and parental status of the married couple.

According to the Obamacare calculator, the extreme case of this tax occurs with a 60-year-old married couple with no children, where the two spouses have identical incomes totaling $62,041 per year. Under this scenario, according to the Obamacare calculator, Obamacare gives them an annual tax of $11,028 for being married instead of single.

61) Obamacare gives people an annual tax increase of up to $12,214 for earning one more dollar of income

In front of the U.S. Supreme Court, the Obama administration argued that Obamacare is a tax.

Obamacare gives some people a <u>tax increase</u> if they increase their income by one dollar. The amount of this tax increase depends upon the person's age, income, and marital status.

According to the Obamacare calculator, the extreme case of this occurs with a 64-year-old married couple with a combined income of $62,041. Under this scenario, according to the Obamacare calulator, Obamacare gives them an annual tax increase of $<u>12,214</u> when their income increases by one dollar, in the case of their income going from $62,040 to $62,041.

This amounts to a marginal tax rate of <u>1,221,400%</u>. That's not a typo - the marginal tax rate on that one dollar of additional income is more than <u>one million per cent</u>.

62) Obama refused to fire IRS employees who "lost" $67 million from "slush fund"

In September 2013, it was <u>reported</u> that IRS employees had "lost" $67 million from a "slush fund." Obama refused to fire those employees. Obama had created the "slush fund" as part of Obamacare.

63) Obama falsely said his mother's insurance company had refused to pay for her cancer treatment

During the 2008 election campaign, Obama <u>falsely</u> said that his mother's health insurance company had refused to pay for her cancer treatment.

64) Obama illegally delayed online registration of Obamacare for small businesses

Obamacare requires that the online registration for small businesses be ready by October 1, 2013. However, five days before that date, Associated Press reported that this deadline would not be met.

65) Obamacare encouraged 30,000 Puget Sound grocery workers to vote in favor of authorizing a strike

In September 2013, a union representing 30,000 employees at Safeway, Fred Meyer, QFC, and Albertson's in the Puget Sound area of Washington state voted in favor of authorizing a strike. Union members said that one of their reasons for voting in favor of the strike was that their employers were trying to switch their part time employees form employer provided insurance to the Obamacare exchanges.

66) Obamacare caused a family's monthly insurance premium to increase from $333 to $965

Andy and Amy Mangione and their two sons live in Louisville, Kentucky. In September 2013, they received a letter from Humana, their insurance company, which said that Obamacare would be causing their monthly premium to increase from $333 to $965.

67) Obamacare caused Michelle Malkin's family to lose their health insurance policy

In September 2013, conservative writer Michelle Malkin, who has always opposed Obamacare, wrote

Like an estimated 22 million other Americans, I am a self-

*employed small-business owner who buys health insurance for
my family directly on the individual market. We have a high-
deductible PPO plan that allows us to choose from a wide range
of doctors.*

Or rather, we had such a plan.

*Last week, our family received notice from Anthem BlueCross
BlueShield of Colorado that we can no longer keep the plan we
like because of "changes from health care reform (also called the
Affordable Care Act or ACA)." The letter informed us that "(t)o
meet the requirements of the new laws, your current plan can no
longer be continued beyond your 2014 renewal date."*

*This isn't just partisan business. It's personal. Our cancellation
letter states that Anthem is "not going to be selling new individual
PPO plans." When we asked whether we could keep our
children's doctors, an agent for Anthem told my husband and me
she didn't know.*

68) **Obama tried to force Little Sisters of the Poor and other Catholic organizations to violate their religious principles**

In September 2013, Becket Fund for Religious Liberty <u>sued</u> the
Obama administration on behalf of Little Sisters of the Poor, a
Catholic charity. Other Catholic organizations were also
represented in the lawsuit.

Sister Loraine Marie <u>said</u> of this lawsuit:

*"We cannot violate our vows by participating in the government's
program to provide access to abortion-inducing drugs."*

Mark Rienzi, one of the lawyers representing these Catholic organizations, said:

"These women just want to take care of the elderly poor without being forced to violate the faith that animates their work. The money they collect should be used to care for the poor like it always has -- and not to pay the IRS."

69) By signing Obamacare, Obama broke his promise not to increase taxes on families making less than $250,000 a year

On September 12, 2008, Obama promised:

"I can make a firm pledge. Under my plan, no family making less than $250,000 a year will see any form of tax increase. Not your income tax, not your payroll tax, not your capital gains taxes, not any of your taxes."

In 2010, Obama signed Obamacare.

In 2012, in front of the U.S. Supreme Court, the Obama administration argued that Obamacare is a tax.

70) Obamacare pushes millions of working people "into a regulatory health coverage no man's land"

In February 2013, U.S. Senator Ron Wyden (Democrat-Oregon) said:

"We've got millions of people — working-class, middle-class people — who are going to be pushed into a regulatory health

coverage no man's land. They are unable to afford the family coverage through their employer and ineligible for the subsidy that could be used by dependents on the exchange."

71) It's "not fair" to force federal lawmakers and their aides to participate in the same health care reform as everyone else

In June 2013, U.S. Congressman John Larson (Democrat-Connecticut) said that it is "not fair" to force federal lawmakers and their aides to participate in the same health care reform as everyone else.

72) SEIU union went on strike over Obamacare

The Service Employees International Union supported Obama in both elections, and also supported the passage of Obamacare.

However, in September 2013, member of the Chicago chapter of the SEIU went on strike over jobs cuts that were caused by Obamacare.

73) Obamacare website removed its promise of "free" health care

In September 2013, the Obamacare website removed its promise of "free" health care.

74) MSNBC host Ed Schultz supports Obamacare but wants unions to be exempt from it

After Obamacare was passed, MSNBC host Ed Schultz praised it almost every day for three years. However, on Sepotember 26, 2013, just five days before the Obamacare exchanges were to begin, Schultz said that unions should be exempt from it.

75) Obamacare punishes people who are unable to accurately predict their income a year in advance

Obamacare requires people to predict their income a year in advance. If their prediction is wrong, they can be punished by the IRS.

76) Less than 1% of the people who visited the Obamacare website on its first day actually registered for Obamacare

U.S. Congressman Congressman Jim Himes (Democrat-Connecticut) said that out of the 28,000 people from Connecticut who had visited the Obamacare website on its first day, only 167 had actually signed up for Obamacare.

77) Obama administration falsely said it did not know how many people had enrolled in Obamacare

On October 3, 2013, the third day that the Obamacare website was in operation, White House spokesman Jay Carney said that "7 million" people had visited the Obamacare website so far. However, when asked how many of those people had actually enrolled in Obamacare, he said, "We don't have that data."

Carney was lying. Of course the Obama administration had that data. CBS News was able to get a copy of that data, and reported that during the first 24 hours after the Obamacare website went online, only six people had used the website to enroll in

Obamacare.

78) The Obama administration broke its promise that Obamacare "navigators" would not go door to door

On October 1, 2013, the very first day that Obamacare registration was taking place, the Obama administration broke its promise that Obamacare "navigators" would not go door to door.

79) Reporters from various news agencies were unable to register at the Obamacare website

On October 1, 2013, a CNN reporter was unable to register at the Obamacare website.

On October 1, 2013, an MSNBC reporter was unable to register at the Obamacare website.

On October 1, 2013, a reporter from the Tennessean was unable to register at the Obamacare website.

80) The Obamacare phone line was answered by "navigators" who had no training

President Obama signed Obamacare in March 2010. The Obama administration had three and a half years to hire and train the "navigators" who answer the Obamacare phone line.

However, on October 1, 2013, one of the "navigators" who answered the Obamacare phone line said "We have not been trained yet."

81) The Obamacare website can't handle as much traffic as a website which is run by one guy in his pajamas from his apartment

drudgereport.com is run by Matt Drudge, who runs the website in his pajamas from his apartment. I've visited his website just about every day since the late 20th century. It runs very well. His website has gotten as many as 45 million hits per day.

On the first day of the Obamacare website, it had 5 million visitors. It could not handle that amount of traffic.

82) Obamacare "navigators" who answered the Obamacare phone line told people to go to a building that turned out to be empty

Obamacare "navigators" who answered the Obamacare phone line told people to go to a building that turned out to be empty.

83) When spelled out, the Obamacare phone number is "F* YO"**

When spelled out, the Obamacare phone number is "F*** YO."

This is not a complaint on my part. On the contrary, I consider this to be truth in advertising. For once, the Obama administration is telling us the truth about Obamacare.

84) A "lead navigator" for Obamacare falsely said that applicants must provide their credit score

In October 2013, Anne Packham, a "lead navigator" for Obamacare, falsely told applicants that they had to provide their credit score.

85) Obamacare website "looks like nobody tested it"

President Obama signed Obamacare in March 2010. He had three and a half years to create and test the Obamacare website.

However, in October 2013, CBS News quoted Luke Chung, an online database programmer who supports Obamacare, as saying the following about the Obamacare website:

"It wasn't designed well, it wasn't implemented well, and it looks like nobody tested it... It's not even close. It's not even ready for beta testing for my book. I would be ashamed and embarrassed if my organization delivered something like that."

86) Obamacare's first publicized "enrollee" turned out to be a Democratic activist who had not actually enrolled in Obamacare

After the Obamacare website went online, the media tried and tried to find someone who had actually enrolled, but could not find anyone, because the website was so badly designed.

After much searching, they finally reported that they had found someone - a 21-year-old guy from Georgia named Chad Henderson.

On October 3, 2013, the Washington Post reported:

Meet Chad Henderson, the Obamacare enrollee tons of reporters are calling

Ask and, apparently, you shall receive.

Just moments after writing a blog post Thursday morning, about the lack of information on Obamacare enrollees, Enroll America reached out with contact information for Chad Henderson, a 21-year-old in Georgia who had successfully enrolled in coverage on the federal marketplace.

It was a little difficult to reach Henderson, mostly because so many other reporters wanted to talk to him. "I'm supposed to talk to the Chattanooga Times Free Press in a half hour," Henderson said. "And The Wall Street Journal is supposed to call."

Luckily, Henderson managed to squeeze me in for a few minutes. He's a student at Chattanooga State University who lives across the state border in Flintstone, Ga.

Politico <u>reported</u>:

Rare health exchange enrollee gets 15 minutes of Obamacare fame

Chad Henderson, a college student who is one of the few people to have signed up for health insurance on a federal exchange, is having his 15 minutes of Obamacare fame.

But wait.

It turns out that Henderson had <u>not</u> actually enrolled in Obamcare.

In addition, Henderson is actually a <u>member</u> of Organizing for Action, the organization that ran Obama's election campaign.

87) Said it's "unfair" to ask for Obamacare enrollment numbers just one week after Obamacare website went online

U.S. Congressional reperestentative Debbie Wasserman Schultz (Democrat-Florida) is the chairperson for the Democratic National Committee. When a reporter asked her how many people had enrolled in Obamacare during its first week, she <u>said</u> it was "unfair" to ask that question so early.

When a new movie comes out, we know how many people bought tickets in the first week. When a new video game, or a new CD, or a new book comes out, we know how many people bought it in the first week.

But when a news reporter asks "the most transparent administration in history" how many people signed up for its new health care program during its first week, we are told that such a question is "unfair."

88) Declined to idenifty the private contractors who screwed up the Obamacare website

When the New York Times asked the Obama administration to identify the private contractors who had screwed up the Obamacare website, the Obama administration <u>refused</u> to answer.

89) Refused to answer why businesses, but not individuals,

were able to delay the Obamacare mandate for a year

When Jon Stewart asked Health and Human Services Secretary Kathleen Sebelius why businesses, but not individuals, were able to delay the Obamacare mandate for a year, Sebelius refused to answer.

90) Gave people Obamacare "rate shock"

Many news sources, including the Washington Post, the Christian Science Monitor, Investor's Business Daily, the Daily Caller, CBS News, Forbes, CNN, the San Jose Mercury News, and the San Francisco Chronicle, have been reporting on something called Obamacare "rate shock."

For example, Tom Waschura, a self employed engineer who lives in Portola Valley, California, said that he supports Obamacare, and that he voted for Obama in both elections.

However, on October 5, 2013, Waschura said:

"I was laughing at Boehner -- until the mail came today."

"I really don't like the Republican tactics, but at least now I can understand why they are so pissed about this. When you take $10,000 out of my family's pocket each year, that's otherwise disposable income or retirement savings that will not be going into our local economy."

This next quote is one of the funniest things that I've heard anyone say about Obamacare so far. It comes from Cindy Vinson, a retired teacher from San Jose, California, who said that she supports Obamacare, and that she voted for Obama in both elections. This is what she <u>said</u> in October 2013, after she found out that Obamacare would be causing her insurance premium to increase:

"Of course, I want people to have health care. I just didn't realize I would be the one who was going to pay for it personally."

CNN <u>reported</u>:

One North Carolina reader was upset to learn her current $267 a month plan was being canceled and the cheapest option on the exchange would cost her family $750 a month. They don't qualify for a subsidy.

"Obamacare is a nightmare for my family," she wrote.

91) Made sure that Obamacare "rate shock" did not happen until after the 2012 election

Obamacare was deliberately written so that Obamacare "rate shock" would not occur until <u>after</u> the 2012 election.

On October 9, 2013, Obama's <u>approval</u> rating was only 37%. Obamacare "rate shock" was a significant factor in this low approval rating. If Obamacare "rate shock" had happened in October 2012 instead of in October 2013, it's highly unlikley that Obama would have won the 2012 election.

92) Obama had the Obamacare website built by cronies instead of by qualified programmers

Obama had the Obamacare website built by <u>cronies</u> instead of by qualified programmers.

93) **Obama used 55 different contractors to build the Obamacare website**

Instead of choosing just one contractor or a few contractors who could properly build the Obamacare website, Obama <u>decided</u> to spread the work out over 55 different contractors, which made it much harder to get all the parts to run together properly.

94) **Obama waited until after the 2012 election to issue major rules for the Obamacare website**

Obama signed the Obamacare law in March 2010. The law requires the online exchanges to be up and running by October 2013. So Obama had three and a half years to get the website ready.

However, Obama <u>waited</u> until after the 2012 election to release some of the major rules for how the website was supposed to be designed. So instead of having three and a half years to get the website ready, Obama made sure the programmers had less than one year.

95) **New York Times reporter was never able to log in to Obamamacare website during more than 40 attempts over 11 days**

During more than 40 attempts to log in to the Obamacare website over a period of 11 days beginning on October 1, 2013, a New York Times reported was <u>never</u> able to log in.

96) Obama hired an illegal immigrant to work as an Obamacare "navigator"

Obama <u>hired</u> an illegal immigrant to work as an Obamacare "navigator."

97) Obama hired someone with an outstanding arrest warrant to work as an Obamacare "navigator"

Obama hired someone with an outstanding <u>arrest</u> warrant to work as an Obamacare "navigator."

98) Obama spent more than $500 million to build unusable Obamacare website

Obama spent <u>more</u> than $500 million of taxpayers' money to build the unusable Obamacare website.

99) Obama refused to fire Kathleen Sebelius, even after the failure of the Obamacare website

Even after the Obamacare website failed, Obama still <u>refused</u> to fire Secretary of Health and Human Services Kathleen Sebelius.

100) There is "no reasonable expectation of privacy" at Obamacare website

The source code for the Obamacare website <u>states</u>:

"You have no reasonable expectation of privacy regarding any communication or data transiting or stored on this information

system. At any time, and for any lawful Government purpose, the government may monitor, intercept, and search and seize any communication or data transiting or stored on this information system. Any communication or data transiting or stored on this information system may be disclosed or used for any lawful Government purpose."

101) Obamacare website requires users to reveal private info before shopping

Legitimate shopping websites such as amazon.com allow users to browse merchandise without having to enter their personal information. However, the Obamacare website <u>requires</u> users to enter their name, social security number, and other personal information before they are allowed to look at the insurance plans.

102) Obamacare website is "a hacker's wet dream"

John McAfee, the computer programmer who founded McAfee, Inc., <u>said</u> the Obamacare website is "a hacker's wet dream."

103) Obamacare caused a leukemia patient to lose his insurance

Michael Cerpok lives in Fountain Hills, Arizona. He has <u>leukemia</u>.

In 2012, his health care cost more than $350,000. But because he had <u>insurance</u>, he only had to pay $4,500 of that amount.

However, in October 2013, his insurance company sent him a

letter which said that because of Obamacare, his insurance policy would be canceled on January 1, 2014.

104) Obama added 11 million words of regulations to Obamacare, which is 30 times as many words as the law itself

The regulations that Obama addded to Obamacare after he signed it are 11 million words long. That's 30 times as many words as the actual Obamacare law that Obama signed in March 2010. Because Obama added these 11 million words without approval from Congress, his actions are illegal.

105) Obama changed the Obamacare registration deadline at the last minute

For three and a half years, the Obama administration repeatedly said that people had to register for Obamacare by March 31, 2014.

However, in October 2013, the Obama administration changed that deadline to February 14, 2014.

106) Obama ignored the successful methods of eHealthInsurance.com

The website eHealthInsurance.com has been successfully selling health insurance since 1998. The website is simple and easy to use.

However, when Obama created the Obamacare website, he chose to ignore the successful methods that are used by eHealthInsurance.com.

**107) For two weeks, CNN reporter was never able to log in to
Obamacare website**

During the first two weeks of October 2013, a reporter from CNN
repeatedly tried to log in to the Obamacare website, and was
never able to log in.

**108) Referred people to uncertified Obamacare "navigagtors"
and "assisters"**

In October 2013, the Obamacare website referred people to
uncertified "navigagtors" and "assisters."

**109) While the Obamacare website was not working, 700
counterfeit Obamacare websites were working**

It's not Obama's fault that criminals created 700 counterfeit
Obamacare websites. However, it is interesting to note that while
the Obamacare website was not working, those 700 counterfeit
websites were working.

**110) Asked Blue Cross Blue Shield not to release Obamacare
exchange numbers**

On October 22, 2013, three weeks after the failed Obamacare
website went online, the Obama administration asked Blue Cross
Blue Shield not to release information on the number of people
who had signed up for their policies through the Obamacare
website.

**111) 100% of Senate Democrats up for reelection planned to
support a delay in Obamacare's individual mandate**

On October 23, 2013, CNN's Dana Bash <u>tweeted</u>:

"new: senior dem source tells me to expect every sen dem running in 2014 to back @JeanneShaheen proposal to delay #ACA enrollment deadline"

112) Obamacare website gave wrong prices

In October 2013, CBS News <u>reported</u>:

A new online feature can dramatically underestimate the cost of insurance.

In some cases, people could end up paying double of what they see on the website.

Industry executives CBS News spoke with could not believe the government is providing these estimates, which they said were useless and could easily mislead consumers. They also said that the website repeatedly states the actual prices could be lower, but it makes no mention that they could be higher.

113) Obamacare website sent false information to insurance companies

In October 2013, it was <u>reported</u> that the Obamacare website was sending false information to insurance companies

114) Threatened to punish people for not buying health insurance from a website that wasn't even working

The Obama administration <u>threatened</u> to impose tax penalties on people who did not buy health insurance from the Obamacare website, even though the website was not working.

115) In the first two weeks of the Obamacare website, "no more than 5,000" enrollees had successfully completed the enrollment process

Two weeks after the Obamacare website went online, it was <u>reported</u> that "no more than 5,000" enrollees had successfully completed the enrollment process.

116) Falsely said "No one is more frustrated than I am" regarding the Obamacare website

On October 21, 2013, regarding the failure of the Obamacare website, Obama <u>said</u>:

"No one is more frustrated than I am."

Obama has absolutely no right to be "frustrated" about any of the Obamacare webstie's problems, because he is the person who chose to cause those problems in the first place.

It was Obama who signed a <u>2,600 page</u> law that he hadn't read.

It was Obama who added an additional <u>20,000 pages</u> of regulations that he hadn't read to Obamacare without Congressional approval.

It was Obama who chose to hire <u>cronies</u> instead of competent programmers to create the Obamacare website.

It was Obama who <u>waited</u> until after the 2012 election to issue some of the main rules for the Obamacare website, which gave the programmers less than one year to comply with those rules, instead of the three and half years they would have had if Obama hadn't waited.

It was Obama who <u>falsely</u> said that the price of annual family insurance premiums would fall by $2,500.

It was Obama who <u>falsely</u> told people that they could keep their insurance if they were happy with it.

It was Obama who <u>gave</u> employers a huge financial incentive to switch their full time employees to a part time, 29 hour week.

It was Obama who <u>refused</u> to fire Secretary of Health and Human Services Kathleen Sebelius after the Obamacare website failed.

Every thing that's bad about the Obamacare website is the direct result of choices that Obama made.

Obama has no right to be "frustrated" at the website's failure.

You want to know the people who really do have the right to be "frustrated" at Obamacare's problems? It's the people who have opposed Obamacare from the start. It's the people who predicted that these problems would happen. It's the people who called the bluff from the very start on Obama's many lies about Obamacare. These are the people who have the right to be "frustrated" at Obamacare's problems.

And yet somehow, not only does Obama falsely say that he is "frustrated," but he also falsely says that he is more frustrated than anyone else.

The people who are truly "frustrated" are the millions of people who were against Obamacare but are now being forced to participate in it.

Obama owns this - he created it. He has no right to be "frustrated" about it.

117) Obamacare website was built using 10-year-old technology

The Obamacare website was built using 10-year-old technology.

118) Obamacare website violates copyright laws

The Obamacare website violates copyright laws.

119) Repeatedly promised that the Obamacare website would be ready on October 1, 2013

This video shows Kathleen Sebelius, Obama's Secretary of Health and Human Services, repeatedly promising that the Obamacare website would be ready on October 1, 2013.

120) Called the Obamacare website "the easiest, most consumer friendly website to use"

Beginnging at 0:44 in this video, Kathleen Sebelius,

Obama's Secretary of Health and Human Services, calls the Obamacare website "the easiest, most consumer friendly website to use."

121) Obamacare website had between 10 and 20 times as many lines of code as it should have had

The Obamacare website has 500 million lines of code.

Dave Kennedy, the CEO of information-security company Trusted Sec, said that a website for a project on the scale of Obamacare should actually have between 25 million and 50 million lines of code.

122) Jared Polis opposes delaying Obamacare's individual mandate for the entire country, but favors such a delay for his own district

U.S. Congressional representative Jared Polis (Democrat-Colorado) voted against delaying Obamacare's individual mandate for the entire country, but later requested such a delay for his own district.

When Polis requested a special delay for his own district, he said:

"We will be encouraging a waiver. It will be difficult for Summit County residents to become insured. For the vast majority, it's too high a price to pay."

123) Gave a no-bid contract to CGI Federal to build the Obamacare website

Obama gave a no-bid contract to CGI Federal to build the Obamacare website.

124) Broke promise to have Spanish version of Obamacare website up and running on October 1, 2013

Obama broke his promise to have a Spanish version of the Obamacare website up and running by October 1, 2013.

125) Broke promise that Spanish version of Obamacare website would be up and running by "mid October" 2013

After Obama broke his promise to have the Spanish version of the Obamacare website up running by October 1, 2013, his administration made a new promise to have it up and running by "mid-October." However, Obama broke that promise too - as of October 25, 2013, the Spanish version of the website was still not up and running.

126) Fired an Obamcare phone operator for truthfully answering a caller's question

In October 2013, a caller to the Obama phone line asked:

"Have you ever gotten anyone who really likes it yet?"

The phone operator, a woman named Earline Davis, answered:

"Um, not really."

Davis was fired for her answer.

127) Gave contract for Obamacare website to Michelle Obama's college classmate

Instead of having the Obamacare website built by someone who was qualified, Obama had it built by CGI Federal, a company that was run by Toni Townes-Whitley, who attended Princeton University with Michelle Obama.

128) Spent $634 million for Obamacare website as of October 1, 2013, even though it was only supposed to cost $94 million

The Obamacare website was originally supposed to cost $94 million. However, when it went online on October 1, 2013, it had already cost $634 million.

129) New York Times writer gave Obama a grade of 'F' for rollout of Obamacare website

On October 25, 2013, New York Times writer Uwe E. Reinhardt wrote:

"... who exactly should be assigned the F for the troubled rollout of HealthCare.gov?"

"Once elected, a president becomes chief executive of a giant federal enterprise. Anyone familiar with corporate management would have thought that for as ambitious and technically a complex project as the initial rollout of HealthCare.gov – so important to many uninsured Americans and so politically important to the White House – the chief executive would have remained in very close touch with the management team overseeing the project and thus would have been briefed daily or

*at least weekly on the progress of the project and especially on
any problems with it."*

*"... the blame for the disastrous rollout of HealthCare.gov goes to
its entire management team, to be sure, but primarily to the chief
executive on top of that project. In my view, not only the
proverbial buck stops on the chief executive's desk, but, for the
management of this particular project, the grade of F goes there
as well."*

130) Said "Don't believe what you've heard" regarding criticism of Obamacare

On October 25, 2013, regarding the various criticisms of
Obamacare, Health and Human Services secretary Kathleen
Sebelius said:

"Don't believe what you've heard."

In other words, the Obama administration says we shouldn't
believe the Washington Post, the New York Times, the San
Francisco Chronicle, Associated Press, Reuters, CNN, MSNBC,
ABC, CBS, NBC, PBS, NPR, Politico, the Wall St. Journal, the
Christian Science Monitor, Investor's Business Daily, Forbes, the
BBC, Huffington Post, the Nation, Mother Jones, or New
Republic.

131) Obamacare requires law abiding citizens to purchase coverage for treatment for heroin addiction

Obamacare requires law abiding citizens to purchase coverage for
treatment for heroin addiction.

132) **Obamacare requires men to purchase coverage for maternity care**

Obamacare requires <u>men</u> to purchase coverage for maternity care.

133) **Obamacare website could not even handle "just a few hundred people" at the same time**

The Washington Post <u>reported </u>that during testing, the Obamacare website could not even handle "just a few hundred people" at the same time.

134) **Obama administration falsely blamed the Obamacare webstie's problems on too much traffic**

The Obama administration <u>blamed</u> the problems of the Obamacare website on too much traffic.

However, the Washington Post <u>reported </u>that during testing, the Obamacare website could not even handle "just a few hundred people" at the same time.

In addition, CBS News <u>quoted</u> Luke Chung, an online database programmer who supports Obamacare, as saying the following about the Obamacare website:

"It wasn't designed well, it wasn't implemented well, and it looks like nobody tested it… It's not even close. It's not even ready for beta testing for my book. I would be ashamed and embarrassed if my organization delivered something like that."

135) "Health insurance cancellation notices soar above Obamacare enrollment rates"

On October 24, 2013, the Daily Caller reported:

Health insurance cancellation notices soar above Obamacare enrollment rates

Hundreds of thousands of Americans who purchase their own health insurance have received cancellation notices since August because the plans do not meet Obamacare's requirements.

The number of cancellation notices greatly exceed the number of Obamacare enrollees.

136) On October 28, 2013, the Obama administration was still falsely claiming that people could keep their insurance

Even as late as October 28, 2013, the Obama administration was still falsely claiming that people could keep their insurance if they liked it.

137) Kathleen Sebelius falsely said that Obama did not know about the Obamacare website's problems before October 1, 2013

On October 22, 2013, Health and Human Services Secretary Kathleen Sebelius said that Obama did not know about the Obamacare website's problem's before October 1, 2013.

However, on October 30, 2013, CNN reported that Obama had

known about the defective Obamacare website a month before it
went online.

**138) Before Kathleen Sebelius ran Obamacare website, she
had long track record of failure at running websites in Kansas**

In October 2013, the Daily Caller reported that before Obama
hired Kathleen Sebelius to run the Obamacare website, she had
had a long track record of failure at running websites when she
was governor of Kansas.

Kansas state representative Scott Schwab said of this:

*"We pretty much expected HealthCare.gov to fail, because she
has a pattern of failing on these big initiatives."*

**139) Federal employees who tested Obamacare website gave it
their approval**

Federal employees who had tested the Obamacare website before
October 1, 2013, gave it their approval.

**140) Obama said he was "mad" over botched Obamacare
website, but refused to fire anyone**

Obama said he was "mad" over the botched Obamacare website,
but refused to actually fire anyone over it.

**141) Kathleen Sebelius said "I don't work for" the people
whose taxes pay her salary**

On October 24, 2013, Health and Human Services secretary Kathleen Sebelius said:

"The majority of people calling for me to resign I would say are people who I don't work for."

142) Obamacare website had only six enrollments in the first 24 hours

During the first 24 hours after the Obamacare website went online, only six people used the website to enroll in Obamacare.

143) Obama falsely blamed insurance companies for canceling policies that did not meet Obamacare's minimum requirements

Obamacare requires all insurance policies to cover pre-existing conditions, maternity care, treatment for heroin addiction, and certain other things.

Therefore, based on simple logic, any policies that do not cover these things are rendered illegal by Obamacare, and must be canceled.

The Washington Post said of this:

"Beginning Jan. 1, the new plans must cover 10 essential benefits including pediatric care, prescription drugs, mental-health services and maternity care. In general, policies that don't offer those can't be sold after 2013."

However, after insurance companies canceled these policies, Obama blamed the cancellations on the insurance companies instead of on Obamacare.

144) Obama administration told insurance company executives not to criticize Obamacare

On October 30, 2013, CNN reported that the Obama administration had told insurance company executives not to criticize Obamacare.

145) In July 2010, Obama knew that Obamacare would cause millions of people to lose their insurance, but he continued to falsely say they could keep it

On October 28, 2013, NBC reported that in July 2010, Obama had known that Obamacare would cause millions of people to lose their insurance, but that he continued to falsely say that they could keep it.

146) Obamacare covers "a narrow network of doctors and hospitals"

On October 29, 2013, CNN reported that Obamacare covers "a narrow network of doctors and hospitals."

147) Obama knew about the defective Obamacare website a month before it went online, but he let it go online anyway

On October 30, 2013, CNN reported that Obama had known about the defective Obamacare website a month before it went online.

148) Valerie Jarrett falsely said "Nothing in Obamacare forces people out of their health plans"

On October 28, 2013, Valerie Jarrett, Obama's senior advisor, tweeted:

"Nothing in Obamacare forces people out of their health plans."

However, the very next day, CBS News reported:

CBS News has learned more than two million Americans have been told they cannot renew their current insurance policies -- more than triple the number of people said to be buying insurance under the new Affordable Care Act, commonly known as Obamacare.

149) Kathleen Sebelius said the Obamacare website "has never crashed" at the exact same time that it was crashing

On October 30, 2013, while giving federal testimony on the Obamacare website, Health and Human Services Secretary Kathleen Sebelius said that the Obamacare website

"has never crashed."

However, at the exact same time that Sebelius was making her statement, the Obamacare website said:

"The system is down at the moment."

"We are experiencing technical difficulties and hope to have them

resolved soon. Please try again later."

150) **"Top Hospitals Opt Out of Obamacare"**

On October 30, 2013, U.S. News and World Report reported that "Top Hospitals Opt Out of Obamacare"

151) **Obama falsely said that using the Obamacare website would be like shopping at amazon.com**

Before the Obamacare website went online, Obama falsely said that using it would be like shopping at amazon.com.

152) **Obama said Obamacare could cause premiums to "fall by as much as 3,000%"**

At 1:17 in this video, Obama says:

"your employer, it's estimated, would see premiums fall by as much as 3,000%"

153) **Obamacare website sent some people the eligibility letters of other people**

In November 2013, it was reported that the Obamacare website had sent some people the eligibility letters of other people - people who were total strangers, who lived in other states.

154) **Obama falsely said that his promise of letting people keep their insurance had included the words "if it hasn't changed since the law passed"**

On June 15, 2009, Obama said:

"That means that no matter how we reform health care, we will keep this promise to the American people: If you like your doctor, you will be able to keep your doctor, period. If you like your health care plan, you'll be able to keep your health care plan, period. No one will take it away, no matter what."

However, on November 4, 2013, Obama said:

"Now, if you have or had one of these plans before the Affordable Care Act came into law and you really liked that plan, what we said was you can keep it if it hasn't changed since the law passed."

155) Three people built a healthcare exchange website that works

On November 2, 2013, it was reported that three people in San Francisco - George Kalogeropoulos, Ning Liang, and Michael Wasser - had read about the defective Obamacare website - which had cost $634 million - and decided to try and build their own health care exchange website that actually worked. And they succeeded. Their website actually works. It's located at http://www.thehealthsherpa.com/

156) White House gave itself waiver which allowed the Obamacare website to go online, despite the fact that it was deemed to be a high security risk

Four days before the defective Obamacare website went online, the White House gave itself a waiver which allowed the website to go online, despite the fact that it was deemed to be a high security risk.

157) Obama denied saying that people could keep their insurance even though it was on video from more than 20 different occasions

Obama denied saying that people could keep their insurance even though it was on video from more than 20 different occasions. The video of him saying it more than 20 different times can be seen at https://www.youtube.com/watch?v=JCUpJDzyRnY

158) Obama broke his promise to "call out" people who lie about Obamacare

In September 2009, Obama said:

"If you misrepresent what's in this plan, we will call you out."

However, as of November 2013, Obama has not "called himself out" for lying about what was in Obamacare. He has not "called himself out" for falsely saying that people could keep their insurance. He has not "called himself out" for falsely saying that families' premiums would fall by $2,500 by the end of his first term. He has not "called himself out" on any of his many Obamacare lies that are on this list.

159) Obama gave CGI Federal new contracts after the launch of its defective Obamacare website

CGI Federal is the company that created the defective Obamacare website, which went online October 1, 2013. After that date, the

Obama administration gave <u>new contracts</u> to the company.

160) Obama apologized– not for lying – but for the fact that people believed his lie

On November 7, 2013, NBC News <u>reported</u>:

President Obama said Thursday that he is "sorry" that some Americans are losing their current health insurance plans as a result of the Affordable Care Act, despite his promise that no one would have to give up a health plan they liked.

"I am sorry that they are finding themselves in this situation based on assurances they got from me," he told NBC News in an exclusive interview at the White House.

"We've got to work hard to make sure that they know we hear them and we are going to do everything we can to deal with folks who find themselves in a tough position as a consequence of this."

161) On November 8, 2013, the White House website still said, "If you like your plan you can keep it"

On November 8, 2013, the White House website <u>still</u> said, "If you like your plan you can keep it"

162) Obama used fraudulent accounting to overstate the number of people who had "enrolled" in Obamacare

In November 2013, the Washington Post <u>reported</u>:

Who counts as an Obamacare enrollee? The Obama administration settles on a definition.

The fight over how to define the new health law's success is coming down to one question: Who counts as an Obamacare enrollee?

Health insurance plans only count subscribers as enrolled in a health plan once they've submitted a payment. That is when the carrier sends out a member card and begins paying doctor bills.

When the Obama administration releases health law enrollment figures later this week, though, it will use a more expansive definition. It will count people who have purchased a plan as well as those who have a plan sitting in their online shopping cart but have not yet paid.

163) In June 2010, the Obama administration estimated that 93 million people would lose their insurance because of Obamacare

In June 2010 in the Federal Register, the Obama administration estimated that 93 million people would lose their insurance because of Obamacare.

164) Obamacare czar Ezekiel J. Emanuel said people should skip their free annual Obamacare physical exam because it was "basically worthless"

Before Obamacare was passed, Obama said that it would provide a free annual physical exam for everyone. However, after Obamacare was passed, Obamacare czar Ezekiel J. Emanuel said that people should skip this exam because it was "basically worthless."

165) Five minute CNN video of Obamacare supporter complaining and complaining and complaining about her insurance being canceled

Here's a five minute CNN video of an Obamacare supporter complaining and complaining and complaining about her insurance being canceled: https://www.youtube.com/watch?v=-F0z-Hxi5s8

166) In December 2013, Obama gave unions even more illegal exemptions from Obamacare

In December 2013, it was reported that Obama had illegally exempted some unions from some of the Obamacare fees, without approval from Congress.

167) Obamacare website gave someone's password, address, and social security number to three complete strangers

In November 2013, MKOV reported that the Obamacare website had given the password, address, and social security number of a woman in St. Louis, Missouri, to three complete strangers.

168) Obamacare "navigators" encouraged applicants to lie about their income and smoking

In November 2013, undercover video footage showed Obamacare navigators encouraging applicants to lie about their income and smoking status. A second video with more examples was also released.

169) "4 Things The US Government Accomplished In Less Time Than A Working Obamacare Website"

In November 2013, camharris.us <u>reported</u>:

4 Things The US Government Accomplished In Less Time Than A Working Obamacare Website

From the day that the Patient Protection and Affordable Care Act went into effect to the morning that the federal healthcare exchange went live, 1288 days passed. 3 years, 6 months, and 8 days. In all that time, our federal government could not construct a website that actually worked, and we are still waiting for a final product.

Here are 4 things the United States government accomplished in less time than it has taken to build a working website:

1. We Fought World War I

April 6, 1917-November 11, 1918

1 years, 7 months, 6 days

2. We Fought A Bigger War

December 7, 1941-May 8, 1945

3 years, 5 months, 2 days

3. We Built The Bomb

June 17, 1942-July 16,1945

3 years, 1 month

4. We Orbited A Man Around The Earth

October 7, 1958-February 20, 1962

3 years, 4 months, 13 days

170) During Obamacare's first month, only 106,185 people enrolled

On November 12, 2013, it was reported that during October 2013, only 106,185 people had enrolled in Obamacare. And even this pathetically low number is fraudulently overstated, because it includes people who had left insurance policies in their shopping cart without paying for them. No legitimate online retailer counts unpaid items left in the shopping cart as a sale.

171) Less than 1% of Massachusetts citizens who lost their insurance because of Obamacare have signed up for a new policy at the Obamacare website

On November 9, 2013, the Boston Herald reported:

Just weeks before a Jan. 1 enrollment deadline, state officials admitted yesterday that just 1 percent of the 150,000 Bay Staters facing canceled heath insurance under Obamacare rules have signed up for new plans.

Massachusetts Health Connector officials told the Herald that only 549 applicants — out of the 150,000 Bay Staters forced to switch their health plans to comply with Obamacare rules — are poised to receive insurance through the new system.

172) "The Obamacare Exchange Scorecard: Around 100,000 Enrollees And Five Million Cancellations"

On November 12, 2013, Forbes <u>reported</u>:

The Obamacare Exchange Scorecard: Around 100,000 Enrollees And Five Million Cancellations

HHS has released the official numbers here. The HHS report states that only 26,794 people enrolled in the federal exchange—which amounts to 23 per state per day—and 79,391 enrolled in the state-based exchanges, for a total of 106,185.

In the market for individually-purchased health insurance, more than 4.8 million Americans have received notices that their preexisting plans are soon to be illegal, and will be cancelled. Many more cancellation notices are imminent.

173) Obama told insurance companies to break the law

On November 14, 2013, after insurance companies had canceled policies that did not meet the minimum requirements of

Obamacare, Obama told them to restore these policies. However,
he did this without Congress voting to approve these changes to
Obamacare. The President does not have the legal authority to
change a law that was passed by Congress, without those changes
first being approved by Congress.

**174) Obama falsely said "In the first month alone, we've seen
more than 100 million Americans already successfully enroll
in the new insurance plans"**

On November 18, 2013, Obama said:

*"In the first month alone, we've seen more than 100 million
Americans already successfully enroll in the new insurance
plans."*

In reality, the actual number was 106,185.

**175) Jessica Sanford, whom Obama had cited as an
Obamacare success story, later said she could not afford to
buy an Obamacare policy**

Jessica Sanford is a a self-employed single mother from
Washington state, who earns slightly less than $50,000 a year, and
has not had health insurance for 15 years.

On October 21, 2013, Obama cited Sanford as an Obamacare
success story, because she would be able to purchase an
Obamacare policy for herself and her son for only $169 per
month.

However, a month later, it was reported that the Obamacare

website had quoted the wrong price for Sanford. Her true, actual price was $621. She said that she could not afford this, and that she would just pay the penalty instead.

176) **Video shows students at historically black college complaining that Obamacare caused them to lose their insurance**

Bowie University is a historically black college in Maryland. This video shows students from the college complaining about how Obamacare caused them to lose their insurance: http://www.youtube.com/watch?v=PPuFt6g_0a8

177) **Obama refused to answer question about whether or not people who don't buy insurance should be put in jail**

The Obama administration argued in front of the Supreme Court that the Obamacare mandate was a tax. Obama hired 16,500 new IRS agents to run Obamacare. In this video, ABC News asked Obama whether or not he thinks that people who don't buy insurance should be put in jail. Obama refused to answer the question. Even after the interviewer asked Obama the question a second time, Obama still refused to answer it.

178) **An estimated 70% of California doctors will not participate in Obamacare**

In December 2013, the California Medical Association estimated that 70% of California doctors would not be participating in Obamacare.

179) **California's Obamacare website gave out the contact**

information of tens of thousands of people without their permission

In December 2013, it was <u>reported</u> that California's Obamacare website had given private insurance agents the names, addresses, phone numbers, and email addresses of tens of thousands of people without their permission.

180) Obama made it easy for a future Republican President to give every U.S. citizen a permanent Obamacare waiver, without approval from Congress

The President does not have any legal authority to change the law without those changes first being approved by Congress. However, this list contains many examples of Obama making changes to Obamacare without approval from Congress. Some of these changes involve Obama giving Obamacare <u>waivers</u> to unions who supported the passage of Obamacare. Other changes include Obama <u>delaying</u> certain parts of Obamacare. Obama made these changes illegally, because they were not approved by Congress. With a small number of exceptions, Democrats have not criticized Obama for doing this.

Therefore, in the future, if a <u>Republican President</u> were to give permanent Obamacare waivers to every U.S. citizens without approval from Congress, the vast majority of Democrats would be hypocrites if they objected to it.

181) Obamacare encourages patients to rig the system to rip off doctors, repeatedly, year after year after year

In November 2013, Forbes <u>reported</u>:

Obamacare has... a 90-day grace period. This means people can buy an Obamacare policy, have costly procedures done and then cancel the policy within 90 days. If the cancellation comes during the first 30 days, the insurer is responsible for trying to collect payment, but after that, doctors are on their own. They would have to spend time and money chasing patients for payments. California Healthline reported that deadbeats "would not receive a fine, a premium rate increase or a repayment order. They also would not be barred from purchasing another subsidized plan during the next enrollment period." No other type of health insurance has a 90-day grace period like this.

182) Tech experts said that a properly working Obamacare website should not have cost more than $10 million, whereas the defective version built by Michelle Obama's incompetent Princeton classmate had actually cost $634 million

Instead of hiring competent programmers to create the Obamacare website, Obama hired CGI Federal, a company that was run by Toni Townes-Whitley, who attended Princeton University with Michelle Obama. When the defective Obamacare website went online on October 1, 2013, it had already cost $634 million.

However, David Kennedy, president of the technology firm TrustedSec, said that even if the Obamacare website had worked properly, it should not have cost more than $10 million. Luke Chung, president and founder of the technology firm FMS, said he agreed with Mr. Kennedy.

183) Harry Reid, Barbara Boxer, and several other Democratic Senators who voted for Obamacare, have exempted their own staff from Obamacare

In December 2013, Yahoo News reported:

Harry Reid exempts some of his Senate staff from Obamacare exchanges

One of the biggest public supporters of the Affordable Care Act has reportedly decided that some of his staff should be exempted from the new law.

CNN reports that Senate Majority Leader Harry Reid is the only top congressional leader to exempt some of his staff from having to buy insurance through the Affordable Care Act exchanges.

Yahoo News has reached out to the offices of all 100 U.S. senators to see if any other members have exempted committee staff from the federal exchange. So far, the offices of 42 senators have responded to our inquiry, with 37 saying that the senator and their entire staff will switch over to the exchanges in January.

The offices of Ron Wyden, Tim Johnson, Barbara Boxer, Patty Murray and Thomas Carper, all Democrats, said they were exempting some of their staff. Reid, a Democrat from Nevada, has not responded.

184) **In a contest for videos to promote Obamacare, the Obama administration gave first prize to a video called "Forget About the Price Tag"**

The Obama administration held a contest where it asked people to make videos to support Obamacare. The Obama administration awarded first prize to a video called "Forget About the Price Tag." The video can be seen at http://www.youtube.com/watch?

<u>v=wpRNAkG-Nx0</u>

185) Obama administration broke its promise to have the Obamacare website fixed by November 30, 2013

On October 25, 2013, White House spokesman Jeffrey Zients <u>said</u>:

"By the end of November, the vast majority of consumers will be able to successfully and smoothly enroll through Healthcare.gov"

However, on December 1, 2013, the New York Times <u>reported</u>:

Insurers Claim Health Website Is Still Flawed

The problem is that the systems that are supposed to deliver consumer information to insurers still have not been fixed. And with coverage for many people scheduled to begin in just 30 days, insurers are worried the repairs may not be completed in time.

"Until the enrollment process is working from end to end, many consumers will not be able to enroll in coverage," said Karen M. Ignagni, president of America's Health Insurance Plans, a trade group.

The issues are vexing and complex. Some insurers say they have been deluged with phone calls from people who believe they have signed up for a particular health plan, only to find that the company has no record of the enrollment.

186) Democratic aides who supported the passage of

Obamacare said their new Obamacare premiums are "simply unacceptable"

In December 2013, Politico reported:

Older Hill aides shocked by Obamacare prices

Veteran House Democratic aides are sick over the insurance prices they'll pay under Obamacare, and they're scrambling to find a cure.

"In a shock to the system, the older staff in my office (folks over 59) have now found out their personal health insurance costs (even with the government contribution) have gone up 3-4 times what they were paying before," Minh Ta, chief of staff to Rep. Gwen Moore (D-Wis.), wrote to fellow Democratic chiefs of staff in an email message obtained by POLITICO. "Simply unacceptable."

In the email, Ta noted that older congressional staffs may leave their jobs because of the change to their health insurance.

187) Members of Congress and their staff are exempt from the income limits for Obamacare subsidies that apply to everyone else

Most people are eligible for Obamacare subsidies only if their income is no more than 400% of the poverty level. For a family of four, 400% of the poverty level is $94,200. A family of four with income higher than that amount it not eligible for an Obamacare subsidy.

However, members of Congress and their staff are <u>exempt</u> from this limit. Members of Congress are paid <u>$174,000</u> a year. Because of their special exemption, a middle aged member of Congress who is married and has children, will get a special Obamacare subsidy of <u>$10,000</u>.

188) Obamacare website often doesn't tell insurance companies about customers who "bought" insurance

On December 1, 2013, the New York Times <u>reported</u>:

Some insurers say they have been deluged with phone calls from people who believe they have signed up for a particular health plan, only to find that the company has no record of the enrollment.

189) In New York City, thousands of Obama voting, well educated, upper class professionals complained about losing their insurance because of Obamacare

In December 2013, the New York Times <u>reported</u>:

With Affordable Care Act, Canceled Policies for New York Professionals

Many in New York's professional and cultural elite have long supported President Obama's health care plan. But now, to their surprise, thousands of writers, opera singers, music teachers, photographers, doctors, lawyers and others are learning that their health insurance plans are being canceled and they may have to pay more to get comparable coverage, if they can find it.

"I couldn't sleep because of it," said Barbara Meinwald, a solo practitioner lawyer in Manhattan.

Ms. Meinwald, 61, has been paying $10,000 a year for her insurance through the New York City Bar. A broker told her that a new temporary plan with fewer doctors would cost $5,000 more, after factoring in the cost of her medications.

Roy Lyons, managing director of Marsh U.S. Consumer, an insurance brokerage, said he had heard complaints from physicians, lawyers, pharmacists and optometrists.

Among those affected are members of the Authors Guild; the Advertising Photographers of America; the Suzuki Association of the Americas, a music teachers organization; the Society of Children's Book Writers and Illustrators; the New York City Bar Association; and the New York County Medical Society.

It is not lost on many of the professionals that they are exactly the sort of people — liberal, concerned with social justice — who supported the Obama health plan in the first place. Ms. Meinwald, the lawyer, said she was a lifelong Democrat who still supported better health care for all, but had she known what was in store for her, she would have voted for Mitt Romney.

It is an uncomfortable position for many members of the creative classes to be in.

"We are the Obama people," said Camille Sweeney, a New York writer and member of the Authors Guild. Her insurance is being canceled, and she is dismayed that neither her pediatrician nor her general practitioner appears to be on the exchange plans. What to do has become a hot topic on Facebook and at dinner

parties frequented by her fellow writers and artists.

"I'm for it," she said. "But what is the reality of it?"

190) **Washington state's Obamacare website stole money from people's checking accounts**

In December 2013, KGW reported that the Obamacare website for Washington state had stolen money from people's checking accounts.

191) **Obama illegally ordered insurance companies to cover "customers" who had never paid any premiums**

In December 2013, Obama ordered insurance companies to cover "customers" who had never paid any premiums. Obama's action was illegal because it violated the takings clause of the Fifth Amendment. It was also illegal because he did not have approval from Congress.

192) **Millennials who voted for Obama and supported the passage of Obamacare did not want to purchase Obamacare insurance for themselves**

In December 2013, it was reported that most of the Millennials who had voted for Obama and had supported the passage of Obamacare did not want to purchase Obamacare insurance for themselves.

193) **Obamcare website violated federal security laws**

In December 2013, it was reported that the Obamacare website was in violation of federal security laws.

194) Obama administration refused to answer questions about how many of Obamacare's so-called "enrollees" had actually paid their first month's premium

On December 11, 2013, more than two months after the Obamacare website had gone online, the Obama administration still refused to answer questions about how many of Obamacare's so-called "enrollees" had actually paid their first month's premium. Instead, the Obama administration was still fraudulently counting as "enrollees" people who had put Obamacare policies into their shopping cart without actually paying for them. No legitimate online retailer counts unpaid items left in the shopping cart as sales.

195) Obama illegally delayed Obamacare's online SHOP enrollment by one year

In November 2013, it was reported that Obama had delayed Obamacare's online SHOP enrollment by one year. Because Obama did this without approval from Congress, his action was illegal.

196) Ten different Obamacare "customer service" representatives refused to let cancer survivor Lynn Baklor sign up for Obamacare

Lynn Baklor lives in Maryland, and is a survivor of breast cancer. Over a period of two months, she spoke on the phone with ten different "customer service" representatives from Obamacare, and none of them allowed her to sign up for Obamacare. The

Obamacare website was not working either. A WBAL news report on her situation can be seen at http://www.youtube.com/watch?v=F79acewkZ78

197) **Obama gave out even more illegal Obamacare waivers**

On December 19, 2013, Obama gave exemptions from the Obamacare mandate to people whose insurance had been canceled due to Obamacare. Because Obama gave out these exemptions without approval from Congress, his action was illegal.

198) **Obamacare creates a new 2% tax on every insurance plan**

Obamacare creates a new 2% tax on every insurance plan. This breaks Obama's promise that he would not raise taxes on families making less than $250,000 per year.

199) **Obamacare requires some people to pay 19% of their income for premiums**

In December 2013, the New York Times reported:

A 60-year-old living in Polk County, in northwestern Wisconsin, and earning $50,000 a year, for example, would have to spend more than 19 percent of his income, or $9,801 annually, to buy one of the cheapest plans available there.

200) **Six Democratic Senators who voted for Obamacare complained that it was causing voters in their districts to lose insurance**

In December 2013, six Democratic Senators who had voted for Obamacare wrote a letter to Health and Human Services Secretary Kathleen Sebelius, complaining that Obamacare was causing voters in their districts to lose insurance.

201) Obama administration admitted that the so-called "Affordable" Care Act was actually "unaffordable" for some people

In December 2013, the Obama administration admitted that the so-called "Affordable" Care Act was actually "unaffordable" for some people.

202) 53% of people without insurance disapprove of Obamacare

In December 2013, the New York Times reported:

Americans who lack medical coverage disapprove of President Obama's health care law at roughly the same rate as the insured, even though most say they struggle to pay for basic care, according to the latest New York Times/CBS News poll.

Fifty-three percent of the uninsured disapprove of the law, the poll found, compared with 51 percent of those who have health coverage. A third of the uninsured say the law will help them personally, but about the same number think it will hurt them, with cost a leading concern.

203) Under certain circumstances, Obamacare recipients between the ages of 55 and 64 can have their homes seized by the government after they die

Under certain circumstances, when someone between the ages of 55 and 64 participates in Obamacare, then after they die, the government can <u>seize</u> their home, preventing their children from inheriting it.

204) PolitiFact repeatedly changed its rating of Obama's promise that people could keep their insurance, based on how many Presidential elections he still had left

PolitiFact is a left wing organization that rates the truthfulness of statements made by politicians. Regarding Obama's promise that people could keep their insurance, PolitiFact has given out three different ratings.

In October 2008, when Obama still had two Presidential elections coming up, PolitiFact <u>rated</u> his statement as "true."

In June 2012, when Obama only had one more Presidential election coming up, PolitiFact <u>rated</u> his statement as "half true."

In December 2013, when Obama could no longer run for President ever again, PolitiFact <u>rated</u> his statement as "lie of the year."

In all three of these cases, PolitiFact was rating the exact same statement. So why did they keep changing their rating? The best explanation that I can think of is that as Obama had fewer and fewer Presidential elections coming up, they were willing to be more and more accurate in their ratings. So only when he was no longer able to run for President again, were they finally willing to admit the truth about his statement.

**205) Obama threatened to fine Catholic nuns over
Obamacare's birth control mandate, all the way to the
Supreme Court**

Little Sisters of the Poor is a group of Catholic <u>nuns</u> that runs
hospice care, i.e., medical care for people who are dying.

Obama doesn't like letting these nuns practice their freedom of
religion. He threatened to <u>fine</u> them for violating Obamacare's
birth control mandate, and planned to take his meddling all the
way to the Supreme Court.

**206) Michelle Snyder, the Obama official who oversaw the
building of the defective Obamacare website, announced her
retirement soon after the website's defective rollout**

In December 2013, Michelle Snyder, the Obama official who
oversaw the building of the defective Obamacare website,
<u>announced</u> her retirement. Obama did not fire her. By retiring, she
will be allowed to collect her full pension and benefits.

**207) AmeriCorps "volunteers" support Obamacare but want
an exemption for themselves**

AmeriCorps is a federal agency that pays so-called "volunteers"
to do "charity" work.

In December 2013, it was <u>reported</u> that the insurance that
AmeriCorps provided to its "volunteers" did not meet
Obamacare's minimum standards, and that, as a result, these
"volunteers" may have to pay the Obamacare tax penalty for not
having insurance.

Abby Grosslein, an AmeriCorps "volunteer" who lives in New Orleans, said:

"It would be nice if the government waived the penalty."

Note she she did not say that the penalty was wrong, or that the penalty should be repealed. Instead, she merely wants certain people to be exempt from the penalty. This is typical of the huge number of examples on this list of liberals who support Obamacare for everyone else, but want exemptions for themselves.

208) Obama administration falsely said that it had never set a target of 7 million Obamacare enrollees by March 31, 2014

In June 2013, the Obama administration said that its goal was to have 7 million Obamacare enrollees by March 31, 2014.

However, in December 2013, the Obama administration claimed that it had never said such a thing.

209) Obamacare could force thousands of volunteer firefighter departments to close

In Janaury 2014, it was reported that thousands of volunteer firefighter departments might be forced to close because they could not afford the cost of Obamacare.

210) Obama administration falsely said that 2.1 million people had signed up for private insurance under Obaamacare by the end of 2013

At the end of December 2013, the Obama administration <u>claimed</u> that 2.1 million people had signed up for private insurance under Obamacare. However, this number included people who had left the insurance in their <u>shopping cart</u> without actually paying for it. No legitimate online retailer counts as sales items that people had left in their shopping cart without paying for.

211) Self described "cheerleader" for Obamacare says she can't afford it for her and her son

In January 2014, CBS News <u>reported</u>:

One Oregon mother says that she is unable to afford health insurance for her and her 18-month-old son because it's too expensive.

The woman — who wishes to remain anonymous — tells KOIN-TV that she originally championed President Barack Obama's signature health care law because she thought it would help people in her situation.

"I've been a cheerleader for the Affordable Care Act since I heard about it and I assumed that it was designed for people in my situation," she told KOIN. "I was planning on using the Affordable Care Act and I had done the online calculator in advance to make sure I was going to be able to afford it."

212) Obamacare website can't handle it when someone has a new baby

In January 2014, Associated Press <u>reported</u>:

For now, the HealthCare.gov website can't handle new baby updates

213) Obamacare includes bailouts for private insurance companies

In January 2014, it was <u>reported</u> that Obamacare includes bailouts for private insurance companies.

214) Wal-Mart's insurance was better and cheaper than Obamacare

In January 2014, it was <u>reported</u> that the insurance that Wal-Mart had been giving its employees was better and cheaper than Obamacare.

215) Obamacare makes it far more expensive for parents of disabled children to pay for their health care

The <u>Davert</u> family lives in Bay City, Michigan. They have twins with brittle bone disease.

Under their children's old insurance, the combined expenses for the two children were capped at <u>$2,500</u> per year. However, Obamacare forced their old insurance to be canceled. Under their new Obaamacare insurance, the combined expenses for the two children are capped at <u>$10,200</u> per year.

216) Obama illegally extended the Obamacare enrollment deadline for people with preexisting conditions

In January 2014, Obama delayed the Obamacare enrollment deadline for people with preexisting conditions. Because Obama did this without approval from Congress, his action was illegal.

217) Obama gave illegal Obamacare subsidies to people in the 36 states that did not set up their own state exchanges

Only 14 states created their own Obamacare exchange.

As the Obamacare law was written, it says that Obamacare subsidies are to be given out

"through an Exchange established by the State."

Despite the wording of the Obamacare law, Obama illegally gave Obamacare subsidies to people in the 36 states that did not set up their own exchanges.

218) Obamacare caused Bill Clinton's favorite Washington D.C. restaurant to shut down its buffet

Filomena is Bill Clinton's favorite Washington D.C. restaurant. On January 1, 2014, it shut down its buffet because of Obamacare.

219) Obama illegally delayed Obamacare's rules on equal coverage

Obamacare prohibits private employers from giving better insurance to top executives than to other employees. In January 2014, Obama delayed this provision of Obamacare. Because

Obama did this without approval from Congress, his action was illegal.

220) **In 2013, Obamacare caused a net reduction in the number of people who had insurance**

On January 1, 2014, the Daily Caller reported that during 2013, Obamacare had caused a net reduction in the number of people who had insurance.

221) **Obama administration criticized the Daily Caller for truthfully reporting that in 2013, Obamacare had caused a net reduction in the number of people who had insurance**

On January 1, 2014, the Daily Caller reported that during 2013, Obamacare had caused a net reduction in the number of people who had insurance. On January 2, 2014, the Obama administration criticized the Daily Caller for truthfully reporting this information.

222) **Obamacare website had such horrible security that it was hacked by one person in less than four minutes with nothing but a regular web browser**

In January 2014, hacking expert David Kennedy was able to hack into the Obamacare website in less than four minutes, using nothing but a regular web browser. During that time, he was able to access the private information of 70,000 people.

223) **Obamacare website is exempt from laws that require other websites to report security breaches to their customers**

The Obamacare website is <u>exempt</u> from laws that require other websites to tell their customers when their private information has been breached.

224) Less than one third of Obamacare enrollees were previously uninsured

In January 2014, it was <u>reported</u> that less than one third of the people who had enrolled at the Obamacare website were previously uninsured.

225) Obamacare encourages employers to limit the size of their workforce to no more than 49 employees

Obamacare's <u>employer mandate</u> only applies to employers with 50 or more employees. This gives employers an <u>incentive</u> to <u>limit</u> the size of their workforce to <u>no more</u> than <u>49 employees</u>.

226) Obamacare makes it harder for patients to get knee replacements, hip replacements, angioplasty, bypass surgery, and cataract operations

In January 2014, it was <u>reported</u> that Obamacare makes it harder for patients to get knee replacements, hip replacements, angioplasty, bypass surgery, and cataract operations.

227) Obama made even more illegal changes to Obamacare

In February 2014, the New York Times <u>reported</u>:

The "employer mandate," which was originally supposed to take effect last month, had already been delayed to Jan. 1, 2015, and now the administration says that employers with 50 to 99 employees will not have to comply until 2016 — allowing Democrats to placate business concerns and pushing the issue well beyond this year's midterm elections.

In addition, the administration said the requirement would be put into effect gradually for employers with 100 or more employees. Employers in this category will need to offer coverage to 70 percent of full-time employees in 2015 and 95 percent in 2016 and later years, or they will be subject to tax penalties.

Because Obama did this without approval from Congress, his action was illegal.

228) Obama illegally banned employers from firing any of their employees to avoid the Obamacare mandate

In a February 2014 article about Obamacare's employer mandate, the Washington Post reported that Obama had banned employers from "cutting back on positions just to fall below the threshold." Because Obama did this without approval from Congress, his action was illegal.

229) Obamacare caused sick children in Seattle, Washington, to lose access to doctors

In February 2014, CBS News reported that Obamacare had caused sick children in Seattle, Washington, to lose access to doctors.

In the report, Dr. Sandy Melzer said:

"The exclusion of a major provider like Seattle Children's from a major insurance network in this market is unprecedented... We're seeing denials in care, disruptions in care. We're seeing a great deal of confusion, and at times, anger and frustration on the part of these families who bought insurance, thinking that their children were going to be covered, and they've in fact found that it's a false promise."

The report can be seen here: http://www.youtube.com/watch?v=D0FHI0vFNgY

230) Obama falsely said that Obamacare "will cover every American"

In June 2007, Obama said

"I will sign a universal health care bill into law by the end of my first term as president that will cover every American."

However, in September 2013, the Washington Post reported

"The Congressional Budget Office estimated back in 2012, before the Supreme Court even gave states the option of opting out of the Medicaid expansion, that there would be 27 million people who lacked health insurance coverage under the Affordable Care Act."

231) Obamacare's tax on tanning salons applies to gym members who never use the gym's tanning salons

Obamacare includes a tax on tanning salons, and this tax applies to gym members who never use the gym's tanning salons.

232) **Although Obama sued states for their "racist" requirement of voter ID, Obamacare requires ID**

Obama's Justice Department <u>blocked</u> Texas's voter ID law, claiming that it was "racist." Obama also <u>sued</u> North Carolina for requiring voter ID.

However, Obamacare <u>requires</u> people to provide ID.

233) **Obamacare may cause the government to seize homes from the estates of poor people**

Between 1993 and 2013, the state of California <u>seized</u> $978.5 million worth of assets from the estates of medicaid recipients.

Obamacare <u>requires</u> everyone in the U.S. whose income is less than 138% of the poverty level to enroll in medicaid.

Based on those two pieces of information, it seems likely that Obamacare will result in the homes of quite a few poor people being seized by the government.

In February 2014, the Los Angeles Times <u>reported</u>:

One thing the ACA didn't change was Medicaid's estate recovery rule. Under a law enacted in 1993, states are required to seek recovery from the estates of deceased enrollees for the costs of long-term care, such as nursing-home care. The recovery rule applied to those who received that care when they were 55 and older, or who were permanently institutionalized at any age.

Medicaid eligibility for the expanded programs is based on income alone, which means there might be some new members with low incomes but sizable illiquid estates, such as homes worth hundreds of thousands of dollars.

The prospect of asset seizures raises people's hackles, especially since under the Affordable Care Act, those earning less than 138% of the poverty level may be offered no choice for subsidized health insurance except Medicaid.

On the whole, the estate recovery program hasn't been a big moneymaker for government at any level. Since 1993, California has collected $978.5 million

234) Obama falsely said Obamacare would not cover illegal aliens

In September 2009, Obama said:

"There are also those who claim that our reform effort will insure illegal immigrants. This, too, is false — the reforms I'm proposing would not apply to those who are here illegally."

However, in February 2014, the Spanish version of California's Obamacare website said:

"No temas si eres indocumentado/a y quieres inscribir a tu familia en un seguro médico."

In English, this means:

"Fear not if you are undocumented and want to enroll your family in health insurance."

235) Obamacare requires pizza restaurants to post the calorie counts for 34 million different combinations of pizza toppings

In February 2014, it was <u>reported</u> that Obamacare requires pizza restaurants to post the calorie counts for 34 million different combinations of pizza toppings.

236) Obama illegally gave Massachusetts another Obamacare waiver

In February 2014, Obama <u>gave</u> Massachusetts a three month extension to fix its defective Obamacare website and get people enrolled in Obamacare. This was illegal for two reasons. First, Obama did it without approval from Congress. And second, the Constitution requires that federal law apply equally to every state.

237) Obamacare prevented Chris Dunn, who was in terrible pain, from getting back surgery

In February 2014, it was <u>reported</u> that Obamacare had prevented Chris Dunn, of Sonora, California, who was in terrible pain, from getting back surgery.

238) Obamacare caused leukemia patient Julie Boonstra to lose her insurance

In February 2014, it was <u>reported</u> that Obamacare had caused leukemia patient Julie Boonstra, of Michigan, to lose her insurance. A video of her can be seen here:

239) Obamacare caused lupus patient Emilie Lamb to lose her insurance

In February 2014, it was reported that Obamacare had caused lupus patient Emilie Lamb to lose her insurance, and that her new insurance was costing her an extra $6,000 a year in higher premiums and co-pays. A video of her can be seen here: http://www.youtube.com/watch?v=ZxImgr13N1k

240) More than 12,000 Congressional staffers enrolled in Obamacare's "small-business" exchange even though they did not own or work for a small business

In February 2014, it was reported that more than 12,000 Congressional staffers had enrolled in Obamacare's "small-business" exchange even though they did not own or work for a small business.

241) Obamacare caused cancer patient and Republican U.S. Senator Tom Coburn to lose his oncologist

Tom Coburn is a Republican U.S. Senator from Oklahoma. He voted against Obamacare. He has prostate cancer. In January 2014, it was reported that Obamacare had caused his insurance coverage to be reduced, and his oncologist was no longer covered. Coburn started paying out of his own pocket to continue seeing the doctor who was treating his cancer.

242) Obamacare's 29 hour work week disproportionately hurt women

In January 2014, the New York Times <u>wrote</u>:

A "29er" refers to someone working 29 hours per week, the maximum that an hourly employee can work and still be considered part time by the federal government, as defined under the Affordable Care Act.

Part-time employees do not create a health-insurance requirement or a penalty for their employer, which gives large and small employers an incentive to reduce at least some employees' hours to 29 hours.

I used the Census Bureau's data to put together a sample of people likely to be 29ers over the next couple of years, based on working 30 to 37 hours per week before this year and not having health insurance available through a spouse (if married). Women outnumber men more than 2 to 1 among likely 29ers. The 29ers are also likely to be less than 30 years old.

Naturally, working fewer hours means less pay. By disproportionately reducing women's work hours, health reform may have the unintended consequence of increasing the gap between men's and women's wages and salaries.

243) Some Obamacare "navigators" had been previously convicted of identity theft

In January 2014, it was <u>reported</u> that some Obamacare "navigators" had been previously convicted of forgery. In August 2013, it had been <u>reported</u> that the Obama administration would not be doing background checks on Obamacare "navigators," despite the fact that these "navigators" would have access to people's personal, private, and financial information. Obama considers background checks to be "racist."

244) WTAE shows small business employees complaining about the high cost of Obamacare

WTAE is the ABC TV station in Pittsburgh, Pennsylvania. In this video, they show small business employees complaining about the high cost of Obamacare: http://www.youtube.com/watch?v=UuA2_P-m4Sk

245) "Public Sector Cuts Part-Time Shifts to Bypass Insurance Law"

In February 2014, the New York Times reported:

Public Sector Cuts Part-Time Shifts to Bypass Insurance Law

Cities, counties, public schools and community colleges around the country have limited or reduced the work hours of part-time employees to avoid having to provide them with health insurance under the Affordable Care Act, state and local officials say.

Among those whose hours have been restricted in recent months are police dispatchers, prison guards, substitute teachers, bus drivers, athletic coaches, school custodians, cafeteria workers and part-time professors.

In Medina, Ohio, about 30 miles south of Cleveland, Mayor Dennis Hanwell said the city had lowered the limit for part-time employees to 29 hours a week, from 35. Workers' wages were reduced accordingly, he said.

Lawrence County, in western Pennsylvania, reduced the limit for part-time employees to 28 hours a week, from 32. Dan Vogler, the Republican chairman of the county Board of Commissioners, said the cuts affected prison guards and emergency service personnel at the county's 911 call center.

In Virginia, part-time state employees are generally not allowed to work more than 29 hours a week on average over a 12-month period. Thousands of part-time state employees had been working more than that

To hold down the work hours of school bus drivers, Vigo County has reduced field trips for children and cut back transportation to athletic events. School employees who had two part-time jobs totaling more than 30 hours a week — for example, bus driver and basketball coach — were required to give up one of the jobs.

The Obama administration says "there is absolutely no evidence" of any job loss related to the Affordable Care Act.

The American Federation of Teachers lists on its website three dozen public colleges and universities in 15 states that it says have restricted the work assignments of adjunct or part-time faculty members to avoid the cost of providing health insurance.

The University of Akron, in Ohio, has cut back the hours of 400 part-time faculty members who were teaching more than 29 hours a week, said Eileen Korey, a spokeswoman for the school.

246) Kathleen Sebelius falsely said "There is absolutely no evidence -- and every economist will tell you this -- that there is any job loss related to the Affordable Care Act."

In February 2014, Secretary of Health and Human Services Kathleen Sebelius said:

"There is absolutely no evidence -- and every economist will tell you this -- that there is any job loss related to the Affordable Care Act."

However, in November 2012, in response to the Obamacare's medical device tax, some medical device manufacturers announced plans to layoff employees, including Welch Allyn (275 planned layoffs), Stryker (1,170 planned layoffs), and Medtronic (1,000 planned layoffs).

In February 2014, it was reported that Obamacare's medical device tax had destroyed 14,000 jobs, and prevented an additional 19,000 new jobs from being created.

In December 2012, Al Franken, Elizabeth Warren, John Kerry, and 15 other Democratic hypocrites who supported the passage of Obamacare wrote a letter to Harry Reid, asking him to delay the tax on medical devices, claiming that the tax would hurt job creation in their districts.

247) "Labor union officials say Obama betrayed them in health-care rollout"

In January 2014, the Washington Post reported:

Labor union officials say Obama betrayed them in health-care rollout

Leaders of two major unions, including the first to endorse

Obama in 2008, said they have been betrayed by an administration that wooed their support for the 2009 legislation with promises to later address the peculiar needs of union-negotiated insurance plans that cover millions of workers.

Their complaints reflect a broad sense of disappointment among many labor leaders, who say the Affordable Care Act has subjected union health plans to new taxes and mandates while not allowing them to share in the subsidies that have gone to private insurance companies competing on the newly created exchanges.

After dozens of frustrating meetings with White House officials over the past year, including one with Obama, a number of angry labor officials say their members are far less likely to campaign and turn out for Democratic candidates in the midterm elections.

"We want to hold the president to his word: If you like your health-care coverage, you can keep it, and that just hasn't been the case," said Donald "D." Taylor, president of Unite Here, the union that represents about 400,000 hotel and restaurant workers and provided a crucial boost to Obama by endorsing him just after his rival Hillary Rodham Clinton had won the New Hampshire primary.

Taylor and Terry O'Sullivan, president of the Laborers' International Union of North America, laid out their grievances this week in a terse letter to House Minority Leader Nancy Pelosi (D-Calif.) and Senate Majority Leader Harry M. Reid (D-Nev.), saying they are "bitterly disappointed" in the administration.

248) Part of the Obamacare website was created by a "repressive dictatorship" in Eastern Europe

In February 2014, it was <u>reported</u> that part of the Obamacare website was created by Belarus, a "repressive dictatorship" in Eastern Europe.

249) 70% of California doctors boycotted Obamacare, but California's Obamacare website falsely said they were participating

In December 2013, it was <u>reported</u> that 70% of California doctors were boycotting Obamacare. However, many of these doctors were <u>falsely</u> listed on California's Obamacare website as participating in Obamacare.

250) A self described "complete fan of the Affordable Care Act" who had cancer complained that Obamacare had caused her to lose coverage for her oncologist

Danielle Nelson lives in Aliso Viejo, California. She has non-Hodgkin's lymphoma, a type of blood cancer. After she found out that Obamacare had caused her to lose coverage for her oncologist, she <u>said</u>:

"I'm a complete fan of the Affordable Care Act, but now I can't sleep at night."

251) Obama gave Oregon $304 million to build its defective Obamacare website that enrolled zero people

Obama gave Oregon <u>$304 million</u> to build its <u>defective</u> Obamacare website. As of February 28, 2014, exactly <u>zero</u> people had signed up at Oregon's Obamacare website.

252) Obamacare's medical device tax destroyed or prevented the creation of 33,000 jobs

In February 2014, it was reported that Obamacare's medical device tax had destroyed 14,000 jobs, and had prevented an additional 19,000 new jobs from being created.

253) A convicted terrorist who murdered two people was hired as an Obamacare "navigator"

In Israel, Rasmieh Yousef Odeh was convicted of putting a bomb in a box of candy on a grocery store shelf, which killed two people. In 2013, she was hired as an Obamacare "navigator." Obamacare "navigators" are not subject to federal background checks, because Obama considers them to be "racist."

254) Harry Reid falsely said that "all" Obamacare horror stories were "untrue"

In February 2014, Senate majority leader Harry Read said:

"There's plenty of horror stories being told. All of them are untrue."

You can see him saying it here: http://www.youtube.com/watch?v=mSJOLivL-NU

He was lying. This list contains many true Obamacare horror stories.

255) Congressman Gary Peters threatened to revoke the

licenses of TV stations if they continued airing an anti-Obamacare ad

In February 2014, Congressman Gary Peters (D-Michigan) had his lawyers sent a letter to TV stations, threatening to revoke their licenses if they continued airing an anti-Obamacare ad. The ad can see seen here: http://www.youtube.com/watch?v=Kpjyr1x7mC0

256) **Obamacare caused Catherine Blackwood to lose coverage for her cancer medications**

Catherine Blackwood lives in Virginia Beach, Virginia, and manages the Family Medicine Center. She has cancer. In November 2013, Obamacare caused her to lose her insurance policy that had been paying for her cancer medications. Her new Obamacare policy does not cover her cancer medications.

257) **Obamacare won't let people switch from one Obamacare plan to another**

Andrew Robinson lives in Orlando, Florida. In early 2014, after he enrolled in one Obamacare plan, he changed his mind and decided that he wanted a different plan. Over a period of several weeks, he spent 50 hours on the phone trying to cancel his original Obamacare plan, but was not allowed to do so.

258) **White House falsely said "You can't say the Affordable Care Act has killed job growth"**

In February 2014, White House health care adviser Phil Schiliro said:

"You can't say the Affordable Care Act has killed job growth."

However, in November 2013, in response to the medical device tax that is part of Obamacare, some medical device manufacturers announced plans to layoff employees, including Welch Allyn (275 planned layoffs), Stryker (1,170 planned layoffs), and Medtronic (1,000 planned layoffs).

In February 2014, it was reported that Obamacare's medical device tax had destroyed 14,000 jobs, and prevented an additional 19,000 new jobs from being created.

In December 2012, Al Franken, Elizabeth Warren, John Kerry, and 15 other Democrats who supported the passage of Obamacare wrote a letter to Harry Reid, asking him to delay the tax on medical devices, claiming that the tax would hurt job creation in their districts.

259) A doctor summed up Obamacare in one sentence

In August 2012, Dr. Barbara Bellar of Chicago, Illinois, summed up Obamacare with the following sentence:

"So, let me get this straight (this is a long sentence), we're going to be gifted with a healthcare plan we are forced to purchase, and fined if we don't, which purportedly covers at least ten million more people, without adding a single new doctor, but provides for 16,000 new IRS agents, written by a committee whose chairman says he doesn't understand it, passed by a congress that didn't read it, but exempted themselves from it, and signed by a president who smokes, with funding administered by a treasury chief who didn't pay his taxes, for which we will be taxed for four years before any benefits take effect, by a government which has

already bankrupted Social Security and Medicare, all to be overseen by a surgeon general who is obese, and financed by a country that's broke... so what the blank could possibly go wrong?"

You can see a video of her saying it here:
http://www.youtube.com/watch?v=vdnY8r7_fLw

260) Obama illegally gave Obamacare subsidies to people who bought insurance from somewhere other than the Obamacare website

As it was passed by Congress, Obamacare only gives subsidies to people who buy insurance at the Obamacare website. However, in February 2014, Obama allowed people who bought insurance from somewhere other than the Obamacare website to get these subsidies. Because Obama made this change without approval from Congress, his action was illegal.

261) An estimated 65% of small businesses that already had insurance will pay higher premiums because of Obamacare

In February 2014, it was reported that an estimated 65% of small businesses that already had insurance would pay higher premiums because of Obamacare.

262) Obama illegally gave unions an exemption from Obamacare's "reinsurance" tax

Obamacare includes a so-called "reinsurance" tax. In March 2014, Obama gave unions an exemption from this tax. This was illegal for two reasons. First, Obama made this change without approval from Congress. And second, the Constitution requires that laws apply equally to everyone.

263) Obama illegally delayed Obamacare's minimum standards for certain insurance policies until after the 2016 election

Obamacare's minimum standards for insurance policies were required to take effect on January 1, 2014. However, in March 2014, Obama delayed these standards for certain insurance policies until after the 2016 election. Because Obama did this without approval from Congress, his action was illegal.

264) Obama illegally extended Obamacare's open enrollment period for 2015

In March 2014, Obama extended Obamacare's open enrollment period for 2015. Because Obama did this without approval from Congress, his action was illegal.

265) Unite Here said Obamacare "threatens the middle class with higher premiums, loss of hours, and a shift to part-time work and less comprehensive coverage."

Unite Here is a union that represents 300,000 employees in the hotel and restaurant industries. It supported Obama in both elections.

In March 2014, Unite Here said:

"If employers follow the incentives in the law, they will push families onto the exchanges to buy coverage. This will force low-

wage service industry employees to spend $2.00, $3.00 or even $5.00 an hour of their pay to buy similar coverage."

"... the ACA threatens the middle class with higher premiums, loss of hours, and a shift to part-time work and less comprehensive coverage."

"Obamacare will cost our members the equivalent of a significant pay cut to keep their hard-won benefits."

"... it will inevitably lead to the destruction of the health care plans we were promised we could keep."

266) **Doctor who survived breast cancer said "Under Obamacare, I'd be dead."**

Dr. Katherine Albrecht lives in Nashua, New Hampshire. After she was diagnosed with breast cancer, doctors at her local hospital told her there was nothing they could do for her. So, she went to experts at the Dana Farber Cancer Center in Boston, Massachusettes, who saved her life. She later received follow up care at Cornell Breast Cancer Center in New York City. Her insurance paid for her treatment at both of these out-of-state facilities.

Afterward, her insurance policy was canceled, because it did not meet Obamacare's minimum requirements.

Her new, Obamacare-compliant policy does not cover treatment in Boston, New York, or any other out-of-state medical facility.

She said of this:

"Under Obamacare, I'd be dead."

267) **Obamacare refused to provide insurance to a business which had paid its Obamacare premiums for three months**

United Reported Publishing is a business in Folsom, California. As of March 2014, it had paid its Obamacare premiums for the past three months, but had not received the insurance that it had paid for. When the company called the Obamacare customer service phone number to try to find out why, the Obamacare customer service refused to do anything to help them.

268) **Obama illegally changed Obamacare's medical loss ratio provision**

Obamacare has a medical loss ratio provision which requires insurers to spend at least 80% of premiums on health care. In March 2014, Obama changed this percentage. Because Obama made this change without approval from Congress, his action was illegal.

269) **Democratic Underground's WilliamPitt said Obamacare caused his wife to lose coverage for her multiple sclerosis medicine, and called Obama a "used-car salesman"**

In March 2014, Democratic Underground's WilliamPitt wrote: (I have redacted the vulgar language from the original)

What I've learned about the Affordable Care Act

What I've learned after a three-month war with these fiends: the ACA says the insurance companies cannot deny coverage to those *with pre-existing conditions, which is true as far as it goes. But they can deny coverage for the life-saving medications necessary to treat those conditions. The insurance company I signed up with through the ACA exchange just denied coverage of my wife's multiple sclerosis medication. We're "covered," to the tune of $700 a month...just not for what she really needs.*

A cozy loophole, that.

*F*** you, insurance industry.*

*F*** you, Mr. President, you piece of s*** used-car salesman.*

*From my heart and soul, f*** you.*

270) More than one third of people who receive Obamacare subsidies will have to repay part or all of their subsidy when they do their taxes the following year

In March 2014, it was reported that more than one third of people who receive Obamacare subsidies will have to repay part or all of their subsidy when they do their taxes the following year.

271) Man received $407,000 in medical bills for care that he had received after his Obamacare policy had taken effect

Larry Basich lives in Las Vegas, Nevada. He started paying his Obamacare premiums in November 2013, for coverage that was supposed to start on January 1, 2014. He paid his premiums every month. However, in March 2014, he was billed $407,000 for medical care that he had received during January and February 2014.

272) Obama administration falsely accused Matt Drudge of lying when Drudge said he had just paid his Obamacare tax

Since Matt Drudge runs a business, he pays his income taxes on a quarterly based. However, in March 2014, after Drudge truthfully commented on this, the Obama administration <u>falsely</u> accused him of lying.

273) Obama illegally delayed the Obamacare enrollment deadline

Obamacare sets the enrollment deadline at March 31, 2014. However, a week before this deadline, Obama granted <u>extensions</u>. Because Obama did this without approval from Congress, his action was illegal.

274) Obamacare author said it will cause most employers to stop offering insurance

In March 2014, the New York Times <u>reported</u>:

Why Employers Will Stop Offering Health Insurance

Here's a prediction: By 2025, "fewer than 20 percent of workers in the private sector will receive traditional employer-sponsored health insurance." The source of this claim? Dr. Ezekiel J. Emanuel, in his just-published book, "Reinventing American Health Care."

Dr. Emanuel is an accomplished oncologist, medical ethicist and academic (and contributing opinion writer to The New York Times). And, of course, he's no stranger to politics: He helped craft the Affordable Care Act as a health policy adviser to the Obama administration, when his brother, Rahm, now the mayor of Chicago, was chief of staff.

... he argues, the so-called Cadillac tax on especially generous health plans, set to take effect in 2018, will help pave the way by discouraging companies from offering those plans.

275) California's Obamacare website gave people voter registration cards that were pre-marked as Democrat

In March 2014, it was reported that California's Obamacare website had given people voter registration cards that were pre-marked as Democrat.

276) Obamacare caused a Kansas hospital to layoff 15 employees

In April 2014, it was reported that Obamacare had caused Newman Regional Health hospital in Emporia, Kansas, to layoff 15 employees.

277) Of the 7.1 million people who enrolled in the Obamacare exchanges, only 20% had been previously uninsured

In April 2014, it was reported that of the 7.1 million people who had enrolled in the Obamacare exchanges, only 20% had been previously uninsured.

278) Obamacare caused a woman who was six months pregnant to lose coverage for her obstetrician

Susan Estrich is a law professor at the University of Southern California. In April 2014, she <u>said</u> that Obamacare had caused her pharmacy technician, who was six months pregnant, to lose coverage for her obstetrician.

279) Obamacare caused New York City brain surgery patient to lose all her doctors and anti-pain medications

<u>Margaret Figueroa</u> lives in New York City. She has had four brain surgeries. On January 1, 2014, Obamacare caused her to lose all her doctors and anti-pain medications. Three months later, she <u>said</u>:

"I have been in pain. I've been vomiting. I lost 22 pounds. The pain is unbearable."

280) Obamacare pediatric dental coverage for Scot Vorse's two children covered zero dentists within a 100 mile radius

<u>Scot Vorse</u> lives in Los Angeles, California. He purchased Obamacare pediatric dental coverage for his two children. However, when he searched the Obamacare website for dentists who were covered by his children's policy, it said that there were zero participating dentists within a 100 mile radius.

281) Obama voters in San Francsico area complained that Obamacare does not actually give them access to a doctor

Mountain View, California, is part of the San Francisco area, where Obama won both elections by a huge percentage. In April 2014, Obama voters in this area <u>complained</u> that Obamacare did not actually give them access to a doctor.

282) Obama threatened to veto a bill that would change Obamacare's defintion of "full time" from 30 hours per week to 40

Obamacare's employer mandate only applies to "full time" employees, which Obamacare defines as those who work at least 30 hours per week. This has <u>encouraged</u> many employers to reduce their employees' weekly hours to 29. In response to this, in April 2014, the U.S. House of Representatives <u>passed</u> a bill that redefines Obamacare's definition of "full time" work to 40 hours per week. Obama <u>threatened</u> to veto this proposal.

283) Obamacare forced New Jersey to eliminate its FamilyCare Advantage health care program

In 2008, New Jersaey <u>started</u> running a program called FamilyCare Advantage, which provided affordable health insurance to families. However, in 2014, Obamacare <u>forced</u> New Jersey to eliminate this program.

284) Obamacare patient got rejected by all 96 doctors that she contacted

In an April 2014 article in Ebony magazine, Danielle Kimberly <u>wrote</u>:

As a proud new beneficiary of the Affordable Health Care Act, I'd like to report that I am doctorless. Ninety-six. Ninety-six is the number of soul crushing rejections that greeted me as I attempted to find one. It's the number of physicians whose secretaries feigned empathy while rehearsing the "I'm so sorry" line before curtly hanging up.

285) Ann Coulter said her friend's sister died because of Obamacare

In February 2014, Ann Coulter said that her friend's sister died because she could not afford to get medical care, because her insurance had been canceled because of Obamacare.

286) Obama gave taxpayers' money to Obamacare contractor to hire employees to do nothing

In May 2014, it was reported that Obama had given taxpayers' money to Serco, an Obamacare contractor, to hire employees to do nothing. The more employees that Serco hired to do nothing, the more taxpayer money it got from Obama. At the time of the report, Serco was still hiring new employees.

287) Obamacare customers filed class action lawsuit because even though they had paid their premiums, they did not receive the coverage that they had paid for

In April 2014, a class action lawsuit was filed in Nevada by Obamacare customers because even though they had paid their premiums, they did not receive the coverage that they had paid for.

288) Huffington Post said Obamacare will leave 40 million Americans uninsured

In February 2014, the Huffington Post reported that Obamacare would leave 40 million Americans uninsured.

289) Obamacare is illegal because it originated in the Senate

instead of in the House

The Obama administration <u>argued</u> in front of the Supreme Court that the Obamacare mandate was a tax.

The U.S. Constitution requires all tax bills to originate in the House, but Obamacare <u>originated</u> in the Senate.

290) Obama changed questions in the census to falsely inflate the number of people who gained insurance from Obamacare

In March 2009, Obama <u>moved</u> control of the Census Bureau from the commerce secretary to the White House. Larry Sabato, a professor at the University of Virginia, <u>said</u> of this:

"The last thing the census needs is for any hard-bitten partisan (either a Karl Rove or a Rahm Emanuel) to manipulate these critical numbers... Partisans have a natural impulse to tilt the playing field in their favor, and this has to be resisted."

In April 2014, the New York Times <u>reported</u>:

Census Survey Revisions Mask Health Law Effects

The Census Bureau, the authoritative source of health insurance data for more than three decades, is changing its annual survey so thoroughly that it will be difficult to measure the effects of President Obama's health care law in the next report, due this fall...

... the new questions are so different that the findings will not be

comparable...

An internal Census Bureau document said that the new questionnaire included a "total revision to health insurance questions" and, in a test last year, produced lower estimates of the uninsured. Thus, officials said, it will be difficult to say how much of any change is attributable to the Affordable Care Act and how much to the use of a new survey instrument.

"We are expecting much lower numbers just because of the questions and how they are asked," said Brett J. O'Hara, chief of the health statistics branch at the Census Bureau.

291) Obama illegally created a new Obamacare rule and penalty without approval from Congress

In May 2014, the New York Times reported:

Many employers had thought they could shift health costs to the government by sending their employees to a health insurance exchange with a tax-free contribution of cash to help pay premiums, but the Obama administration has squelched the idea in a new ruling. Such arrangements do not satisfy the health care law, the administration said, and employers may be subject to a tax penalty of $100 a day — or $36,500 a year — for each employee who goes into the individual marketplace.

Obama's actions here are illegal. There is nothing in Obamacare that gives Obama or the IRS the power to prohibit employers from dumping employees onto Obamacare exchanges, or for fining them $100 a day per employee for doing so. The President does not have the legal authority to change the law without those changes first being approved by Congress.

292) Obamacare forced colon cancer survivor Janet Grigg to lose her doctor. Her new Obamacare policy covers zero doctors within a 400 mile radius of her home.

Janet Grigg lives in Oklahoma and is a survivor of colon cancer. Obamacare caused her to lose coverage for her doctor. Her new Obamacare policy covers zero doctors within a 400 mile radius of her home. You can see a video of her at http://www.youtube.com/watch?v=7FoyREgDH_8

293) Obama gave bonuses to employees who created Oregon's defective Obamacare website

Obama gave Oregon $304 million to build its defective Obamacare website. As of February 28, 2014, exactly zero people had signed up at Oregon's Obamacare website.

However, in June 2014, it was reported that the employees who had built Oregon's defective Obamacare website had been given $650,000 in taxpayer funded bonuses.

294) After cancer patient Linda Rolain paid her Obamacare premiums, Obamacare refused to pay for her medical treatment, and she died

Linda Rolain lived in Las Vegas. She had brain cancer. After she paid her Obamacare premiums, Obamacare refused to pay for her medical treatment, and she died.

295) Obamacare call center employee left confidential info of Obamacare customers at a deli

In June 2014, it was <u>reported</u> that an employee of an Obamacare call center had left a backpack containing handwritten notepads at a deli in Hartford, Connecticut. The notepads contained names, addresses, and social security numbers of 151 Obamacare customers.

296) Obama illegally gave Obamacare waivers to U.S. territories

In July 2014, it was <u>reported</u> that Obama had given Obamacare waivers to U.S. territories (Puerto Rico, Guam, the Virgin Islands, etc.,), which exempted them from certain Obamacare regulations. Because Obama did this without approval from Congress, his action was illegal.

297) Obama gave Obamacare policies and subsidies to non-existent people with fake ID

In July 2014, it was <u>reported</u> that Obamacare had given policies and subsidies to non-existent people with fake ID.

298) Obama illegally ignored Obamacare author Jonathan Gruber's comments that subsidies only apply to state exchanges

On January 18, 2012, Jonathan Gruber, a Massachusetts Institute of Technology economist who helped write Obamacare, <u>said</u>:

"What's important to remember politically about this is if you're a state and you don't set up an exchange, that means your citizens don't get their tax credits."

You can see him saying it in this video. Link set to start video at 31:25, the relevant point: https://www.youtube.com/watch?v=GtnEmPXEpr0&feature=youtu.be&t=31m25s

On January 10, 2012, Gruber said:

"… if your governor doesn't set up an exchange, you're losing hundreds of millions of dollars of tax credits to be delivered to your citizens…"

You can hear him saying it in this video. Link set to start at 1:16, the relevant point: https://www.youtube.com/watch?v=LbMmWhfZyEI&t=1m16s

So how is it that the federal government is giving subsidies through the federal exchange?

It's because under the corrupt leadership of President Obama, the IRS illegally gave itself new power without approval from Congress.

299) Obama falsely promised that Obamacare would give people "the same kind of insurance that Senator McCain and I enjoy"

In 2008, Obama said:

"If you don't have health insurance, you're going to be able to buy the same kind of insurance that Senator McCain and I enjoy as federal employees."

However, the New York Times reported:

"No patient gets closer medical attention than the president of the United States. Wherever he goes, a doctor, nurse or paramedic trails a few footsteps behind, ready for any medical need. It is the ultimate in concierge medicine."

300) **46% of doctors gave Obamacare a "D" or an "F"**

In a September 2014 survey by the Physicians Foundation, 46% of doctors gave Obamacare a "D" or an "F."

301) **Obamacare architect Jonathan Gruber said Obamacare was passed due to "lack of transparency" and "the stupidity of the American voter"**

In October 2013, Obamacare architect Jonathan Gruber said:

"This bill was written in a tortured way to make sure CBO did not score the mandate as taxes. If CBO [Congressional Budget Office] scored the mandate as taxes, the bill dies. Okay, so it's written to do that. In terms of risk rated subsidies, if you had a law which said that healthy people are going to pay in – you made explicit healthy people pay in and sick people get money, it would not have passed... Lack of transparency is a huge political advantage. And basically, call it the stupidity of the American voter or whatever, but basically that was really really critical for the thing to pass....Look, I wish Mark was right that we could make it all transparent, but I'd rather have this law than not."

302) **Obamacare architect Jonathan Gruber lied to the New York Times in a disclosure contract that he signed**

In January 2010, the New York Times <u>wrote</u>:

Corrections

January 9, 2010

Editors' note

On July 12, the Op-Ed page published an article by Jonathan Gruber, a professor of economics at M.I.T., on health insurance and taxation. On Friday, Professor Gruber confirmed reports that he is a paid consultant to the Department of Health and Human Services, and that his contract was in effect when he published his article. The article did not disclose this relationship to readers.

Like other writers for the Op-Ed page, Professor Gruber signed a contract that obligated him to tell editors of such a relationship. Had editors been aware of Professor Gruber's government ties, the Op-Ed page would have insisted on disclosure or not published his article.

303) **When M.I.T. economics professor Jonathan Gruber wrote a pro-Obamacare opinion piece for the Washington Post, he did not disclose the fact that the Obama administration had paid him $392,000 to help write Obamacare**

In December 2009, when M.I.T. economics professor Jonathan Gruber wrote a pro-Obamacare opinion piece for the Washington Post, he did <u>not</u> disclose the fact that the Obama administration had paid him $392,000 to help write Obamacare.

304) **Obama ordered Obamacare architect Jonathan Gruber to lie about Obamacare's Cadillac tax**

In July 2009, Obama ordered Obamacare architect Jonathan Gruber to lie about Obamacare's Cadillac tax.

305) **Obama administration falsely said that Obama had never worked with Obamacare architect Jonathan Gruber at the White House**

Although the Obama administration said that Obama had never worked with Obamacare architect Jonathan Gruber at the White House, White House visitor logs show that Obama and Gruber were together in the same room in the White House for nearly four hours on July 20, 2009.

306) **Nancy Pelosi gave Obamacare waivers to 38 restaurants, nightclubs, and hotels in her own Congressional district**

Although Congresswoman Nancy Pelosi (D-California) voted for Obamacare, in April 2011, she gave Obamacare waivers to 38 restaurants, nightclubs, and hotels in her own Congressional district.

307) **Obamacare, when combined with Obama's executive amnesty, gives employers a $3,000 annual incentive, per employee, to hire illegal aliens instead of U.S. citizens**

Obamacare, when combined with Obama's November 2014 executive amnesty, gives employers a $3,000 annual incentive, per employee, to hire illegal aliens instead of U.S. citizens.

308) Obama administration falsely overstated the number of Obamacare signups by incorrectly including dental subscribers

In November 2014, it was reported that the Obama administration had falsely overstated the number of Obamacare signups by incorrectly including 380,000 dental subscribers.

309) After three private companies did exactly what Obamacare told them to do, the Obama administration sued them for violating the Americans with Disabilities Act

Obamacare encourages employers to offer their employees financial incentives to engage in healthy behaviors, such as quitting smoking, losing weight, etc. However, in November 2014, it was reported that the Obama administration had sued Honeywell International and two smaller companies for doing exactly that. The Obama administration claimed that by doing what Obamacare told them to do, they were violating the Americans With Disabilities Act.

310) November 2014 Gallup poll showed that Obamacare made health care less affordable, which is the opposite of what Obama had promised

President Obama signed Obamacare in March 2010. In November 2014, the Daily Caller reported:

Gallup: Peak Number Of Americans Delaying Medical Care Over Costs

One in three Americans has put off seeking medical treatment in

2014 due to high costs, according to Gallup — the highest percentage since Gallup began asking the question in 2001.

Thirty-three percent of Americans have delayed medical treatment for themselves or their families because of the costs they'd have to pay, according to the survey. Obamacare, of course, had promised that it would help make health care more affordable for everyone, but the number of people who can't afford a trip to the doctor has actually risen three points since 2013, before most Obamacare provisions took effect.

The hardest-hit: the middle-class. Americans with an annual household income of between $30,000 and $75,000 began delaying medical care over costs more in 2014, up to 38 percent in 2014 from 33 percent last year; among households that earn above $75,000, 28 percent delayed care this year, compared to just 17 percent last year.

311) Obamacare architect Jonathan Gruber secretly told the Democratic governor of Wisconsin that Obamacare would make premiums more expensive, at the same time that Obama was telling everyone it would make them less expensive

In November 2014, it was reported that in 2010, when Obama was telling everyone that Obamacare would make premiums less expensive, Obamacare architect Jonathan Gruber secretly told Jim Doyle, the Democratic governor of Wisconsin, that Obamacare would make premiums more expensive.

312) California's Obamacare exchange refused to pay Obamacare navigators for work that they had done more than half a year earlier

In November 2014, it was <u>reported</u> that some Obamacare navigators in California had not been paid for work that they had done at the beginning of the year.

313) Obamacare forced some people to buy an Obamacare policy even though they were also enrolled in Medicare

In December 2014, it was <u>reported</u> that some people were being forced to buy an Obamacare policy even though they were already enrolled in Medicare. When these people tried to cancel their Obamacare plans, they were unable to do so.

314) For some families, Obamacare's "affordable" insurance can cost them "almost a quarter of their family income"

In December 2014, NPR <u>reported</u>:

Don Benfield of Taylorsville, N.C., makes $11 an hour...

The situation only gets worse if Benfield decided to add his wife to his employer policy. Adding her would nearly triple the annual cost, driving it up to $6,200 a year, almost a quarter of their family income.

315) Obama administration illegally told employers that they could not dump their sick employees onto Obamacare exchanges

Obamacare <u>allows</u> employers to dump their sick employees onto Obamacare exchanges. However, in December 2014, the Obama administration told employers that they were not allowed to do this. Because Obama made this change to Obamacare without approval from Congress, his action was illegal.

316) "I'm an Obama supporter. But Obamacare has hurt my family. Obamacare has been far more frustrating than I'd ever dreamed."

In December 2014, the Washington Post <u>wrote</u>:

I'm an Obama supporter. But Obamacare has hurt my family.

Obamacare has been far more frustrating than I'd ever dreamed.

By Catherine Keefe

December 10, 2014

Obamacare brought us new health insurance options, but cost us our more affordable plans.

In November 2013, Jim learned his small-business policy would be canceled because it didn't comply with the new mandate to cover pediatric dentistry and maternity care.

The individual plan I had with Blue Cross was canceled, too.

We learned patience, but we couldn't keep our doctors.

We had applied online and sent copies of our passports to California Covered for verification, but we received no bill, no confirmation of our coverage, no insurance cards. Jim spent an hour and a half on hold once before getting disconnected. He tried again the next day, waiting another two hours before getting disconnected.

... the urologist wouldn't accept our new Blue Shield plan – even though the Blue Shield website said he did.

We have no choice to opt out of the required pediatric dentistry or maternity coverage we'll never use...

317) Harvard faculty members who supported the passage of Obamacare later complained that they had to pay for it

In January 2015, the New York Times reported:

For years, Harvard's experts on health economics and policy have advised presidents and Congress on how to provide health benefits to the nation at a reasonable cost. But those remedies will now be applied to the Harvard faculty, and the professors are in an uproar.

Members of the Faculty of Arts and Sciences, the heart of the 378-year-old university, voted overwhelmingly in November to oppose changes that would require them and thousands of other Harvard employees to pay more for health care. The university says the increases are in part a result of the Obama administration's Affordable Care Act, which many Harvard professors championed.

The faculty vote came too late to stop the cost increases from taking effect this month, and the anger on campus remains focused on questions that are agitating many workplaces: How should the burden of health costs be shared by employers and employees? If employees have to bear more of the cost, will they skimp on medically necessary care, curtail the use of less valuable services, or both?

In Harvard's health care enrollment guide for 2015, the university said it "must respond to the national trend of rising health care costs, including some driven by health care reform," in the form of the Affordable Care Act. The guide said that Harvard faced "added costs" because of provisions in the health care law that extend coverage for children up to age 26, offer free preventive services like mammograms and colonoscopies and, starting in 2018, add a tax on high-cost insurance, known as the Cadillac tax.

Richard F. Thomas, a Harvard professor of classics and one of the world's leading authorities on Virgil, called the changes "deplorable, deeply regressive, a sign of the corporatization of the university."

Mary D. Lewis, a professor who specializes in the history of modern France and has led opposition to the benefit changes, said they were tantamount to a pay cut. "Moreover," she said, "this pay cut will be timed to come at precisely the moment when you are sick, stressed or facing the challenges of being a new parent."

Jerry R. Green, a professor of economics and a former provost who has been on the Harvard faculty for more than four decades, said the new out-of-pocket costs could lead people to defer medical care or diagnostic tests, causing more serious illnesses and costly complications in the future.

"It's equivalent to taxing the sick," Professor Green said. "I don't think there's any government in the world that would tax the sick."

"It seems that Harvard is trying to save money by shifting costs to sick people," said Mary C. Waters, a professor of sociology. "I don't understand why a university with Harvard's incredible resources would do this. What is the crisis?"

318) Although Obama said Obamacare would reduce the number of E.R. visits, a Harvard study showed there was actually an increase

Before Obamacare was passed, Obama said it would reduce the number of emergency room visits. However, a study published by Harvard University in January 2014 showed that Obamacare had actually caused an increase in emergency room visits.

319) After Vermont paid Obamacare architect Jonathan Gruber $80,000 for his "research assistants," Gruber refused to provide the names, W-2's, and other information to prove that these "research assistants" actually existed

In November 2014, after Vermont paid Obamacare architect Jonathan Gruber $80,000 for his "research assistants," Gruber refused a request to provide the names, W-2's, and other information to prove that these "research assistants" actually existed.

320) Obamacare architect Jonathan Gruber said "The real substance of cost control is all about a single thing: telling patients they can't have something they want."

In October 2009, Obamacare architect Jonathan Gruber wrote:

"The real substance of cost control is all about a single thing: telling patients they can't have something they want."

Although liberals ignored Gruber's remark, two months earlier, in August 2009, they were very critical of Sarah Palin's claim that Obamacare would result in "death panels."

I don't know if Palin's claim about "death panels" is true or false. But I do know that the liberals who criticized Palin's statement while ignoring Gruber's statement were being hypocritical.

321) Obamacare illegally gave the President powers that were not permitted by the Constitution

In December 2014, the American Spectator wrote:

The Constitution does not permit Congress to cede its legislative powers to any other branch of the government. Yet, this is precisely what the Democrats did in the case of IPAB. Prior to the passage of Obamacare only Congress had the power to make changes to Medicare's payment rates or coverage. But PPACA transferred that power to IPAB, an Executive branch body whose members will be appointed by the President.

322) Julie Moreno borrowed $14,000 to pay for cataract surgery because her Obamacare policy refused to pay for it

In February 2015, it was reported that Julie Moreno of Mountain View, California, borrowed $14,000 to pay for cataract surgery because her Obamacare policy refused to pay for it.

323) Obamacare customer service telephone number connected an Obamacare customer to "someone reading off a script in the Philippines"

In November 2014, a New York Times article on Obamacare <u>said</u> that Health Republic Insurance was

... a new co-op plan created under the law, for people who lived in the area.

In February 2015, the New York Times <u>wrote</u>:

Compounding the problem is the lack of basic information to shop effectively. When Andrea Greenberg, a New York lawyer, called the help line of Health Republic to clarify the difference between two plans, she found herself speaking to someone reading off a script in the Philippines. "I was really outraged," she said. "This is an important decision with potentially dire consequences. It's not like you're choosing a sweater."

324) During the first year that Obamacare was in effect, the percentage of U.S. citizens who said they had trouble affording health care increased from 36% to 46%

In February 2015, the New York Times <u>wrote</u>:

A recent New York Times/CBS poll found that 46 percent of Americans said they had trouble affording health care, up 10 percentage points in just one year.

325) A year after Obamacare took effect, the New York Times wrote, "For still others, the new fees are so confusing and

unsupportable that they just avoid seeing doctors"

A February 2015 New York Times article on Obamacare said:

"For still others, the new fees are so confusing and unsupportable that they just avoid seeing doctors."

326) Although Obamacare gives employers an incentive to reduce their employees' hours, Obama criticized companies that actually responded to this incentive

Because Obamacare's employer mandate only applies to employees who work 30 or more hours per week, it gives employers an incentive to reduce their employees' hours to 29 hours per week.

In July 2013, the New York Times reported that Obamacare

"... sharply penalizes full-time employment in favor of part-time employment."

In July 2013, leaders of the Teamsters, UFCW, and UNITE-HERE sent a letter to Harry Reid and Nancy Pelosi which said that Obamacare will

"... destroy the foundation of the 40 hour work week that is the backbone of the American middle class... the law creates an incentive for employers to keep employees' work hours below 30 hours a week. Numerous employers have begun to cut workers' hours to avoid this obligation."

Although it was Obama himself who signed Obamacare into law in March 2010, in February 2015 Obama said:

"... when I hear large corporations that make billions of dollars in profits trying to blame our interest in providing health insurance as an excuse for cutting back workers' wages, shame on them."

327) **Obama falsely said, "There is no reason for an employer who is not currently providing health care to their workers to discourage them from either getting health insurance on the job or being able to avail themselves of the Affordable Care Act."**

In February 2015, Obama said:

"There is no reason for an employer who is not currently providing health care to their workers to discourage them from either getting health insurance on the job or being able to avail themselves of the Affordable Care Act."

However, in the same article, Reuters explained that there is indeed such a reason:

"The Affordable Care Act requires companies with more than 50 employees to pay for health insurance for people who work 30 hours a week or more. Reuters has reported that some businesses are keeping staffing numbers below 50 or cutting the work week to less than 30 hours to avoid providing employee health insurance."

328) **In February 2015, Democrats who voted for Obamacare**

complained that people actually had to pay for it

In February 2015, Associated Press <u>reported</u>:

Democrats seek relief from health law penalties

Senior Democrats seek sign-up extension for people facing health law penalties

Three senior House members told The Associated Press that they plan to strongly urge the administration to grant a special sign-up opportunity for uninsured taxpayers who will be facing fines under the law for the first time this year.

The three are Michigan's Sander Levin, the ranking Democrat on the Ways and Means Committee, and Democratic Reps. Jim McDermott of Washington, and Lloyd Doggett of Texas. All worked to help steer Obama's law through rancorous congressional debates from 2009-2010.

"Open enrollment period ended before many Americans filed their taxes," the three lawmakers said in a statement. "Without a special enrollment period, many people (who will be paying fines) will not have another opportunity to get health coverage this year.

"A special enrollment period will not only help many Americans avoid making an even larger payment next year, but, more importantly, it will help them gain quality health insurance for 2015," the lawmakers added.

329) Obama gave out even more illegal exemptions to

Obamacare

In February 2015, Obama gave out even more exemptions to
Obamacare. Because he did this without approval from Congress,
his action was illegal.

330) **Obama administration sent false tax information to
800,000 Obamacare enrollees**

In February 2015, it was reported that the Obama administration
had sent false tax information to 800,000 Obamacare enrollees.

331) **"Why This Liberal No Longer Supports Universal
Health Care: An Open Letter to President Obama"**

Melissa Klein lives in San Francisco, California. In February
2015, she wrote:

*Why This Liberal No Longer Supports Universal Health Care: An
Open Letter to President Obama*

Dear President Obama,

*I voted for you in both elections. I'm proud to call you our
president. I was a staunch supporter of universal health care.
Thank you for following through on your campaign promise. That
you did so IS significant.*

*But I have to say, you've let us down in a big way. This health
care system blows.*

For the past few weeks I've been dealing with this 1095-A issue. You see, I never received it and as you know I need it to file my taxes. Being a law abiding citizen and all, I typically like to file my taxes on time.

I called Covered California in January and was assured I'd get it soon. But alas, it never arrived. So, I spent my entire afternoon (and part of yesterday afternoon), on hold with different folks at Kaiser and Covered California.

At first I wasn't worried. I mean, a) I'm insured. b) I have several letters from Covered California congratulating me on being insured. c) I have emails from Kaiser and Covered California confirming payment for insurance. d) I have my credit card bill that also shows that I, in fact, paid for insurance. And e) I'm insured!!!

My second interaction with Covered California on this issue was both straightforward and unhelpful.

"If you didn't receive a 1095-A you have to fill out a dispute form and FAX it to us."

I respond, "Ok, but I'm not disputing anything. I'm asking for the form you're supposed to have sent me."

Alas, my logic seems illogical to the person on the helpline and she tells me that her hands are tied and that nothing can be done until I submit a dispute form.

I sheepishly ask, "Can I email it to you?"

"No, but you can fax it."

Of course I can FAX it. Cuz, we're in 2015. Who doesn't fax stuff?

Miraculously, I manage to find a fax machine and send over my dispute form.

I call back today to make sure that they received my fax.

After being on hold for 30 minutes I'm told, "We'll let you know in 2 weeks if we received the fax. You'll get a letter in the mail."

So I ask again, "Can't you just tell me over the phone?"

"Nope, ya gotta wait for the letter."

I then ask what I think is a simple question. Shame on me. "Can you at least tell me if a 1095 was ever generated?"

This is when things turn from bad to comical.

"Ma'am, it doesn't appear as though you're in our system for having insurance in 2014. Are you sure you didn't imagine signing up through our exchange?"

"I'm sorry ma'am but I think you're mistaken. You signed up through Kaiser and Kaiser will send you the 1095."

Getting through to Kaiser took a mere 48 minutes. But who's counting? Once someone finally picks up I'm told, "Oh yes, I see right here, you were covered by us in 2014 through Covered California."

"But you need to talk to them about the 1095." Of course I do.

And so, I call Covered California back. I'm thrilled to inform them that I didn't imagine signing up through the exchange and that Kaiser can, without a doubt, confirm that I'm covered.

I'm then told, "Ma'am, you need to submit a dispute form."

"I've already done that," I say exasperated.

"Well, they'll figure it out within 60 days. Don't worry you'll still get your taxes filed in time," The women replies matter of fact-ly.

"60 days?," I respond again, exasperated. "Actually, if you're telling me I'll receive my form in 60 days I will have missed the deadline."

"Oh. Sorry about that. You'll have to file for an extension then. Is there anything else I can help you with?"

332) After supporting Obama in both elections, the National Education Association complained that Obamacare's Cadillac tax would "unfairly cause hardship to American workers and their families"

The National Education Association is a teachers union. It supported Obama in both elections. In April 2015, it complained that Obamacare's Cadillac tax would "unfairly cause hardship to

American workers and their families."

333) In March 2015, Democratic U.S. Senators who voted for Obamacare made yet another complaint about Obamacare, and asked for yet another delay to it

A provision of Obamacare says that in 2016, employers with between 51 and 100 employees will be moved from the "large group" market to the "small group" market. In March 2015, Democratic U.S. Senators who voted for Obamacare complained that this move would make insurance more expensive, and asked for it to be delayed.

334) Obama falsely classified the U.S. Congress as a "small business" with "45 employees" so it could collect Obamacare subsidies

In 2013, Obama falsely classified the U.S. Congress as a "small business" with "45 employees" so it could collect Obamacare subsidies.

335) Obamacare punished small business owners who paid directly for their employees' health care

Beginning on July 1, 2015, Obamacare punished small business owners who paid directly for their employees' health care. If a private business had fewer than 50 employees, and the employer paid directly for their health care, Obamacare required the employer to pay a tax of $100 per day per employee.

336) Although the so-called justification for Obamacare is that health insurance constitutes "interstate commerce,"

Obamacare policies are not actually allowed to be sold across state lines

Supporters of Obamacare try to justify it by saying that health insurance constitutes "interstate commerce." However, Obamacare policies are <u>not actually allowed</u> to be sold across state lines.

337) Obamacare's prohibition against selling health insurance across states lines caused insurance premiums to skyrocket

Competition, when it's allowed, keeps prices down. However, Obamacare forces people to buy health insurance in the same state where they live. Obamacare policies are not allowed to be sold across state lines. As a result, there was very little competition, and this caused prices to skyrocket. In October 2015, the New York Times <u>wrote</u>:

Many Need to Shop Around on HealthCare.gov as Prices Jump, U.S. Says

In Tennessee, the state insurance commissioner approved a 36 percent rate increase for the largest health insurer in the state's individual marketplace. In Iowa, the commissioner approved rate increases averaging 29 percent for the state's dominant insurer....

... only one insurer is offering coverage in the marketplace in Wyoming, and consumers have a choice of just two insurers in Alaska, Hawaii, Oklahoma, South Dakota and West Virginia....

In Minnesota, officials approved increases averaging 49 percent for Blue Cross and Blue Shield of Minnesota...

The Iowa insurance commissioner, Nick Gerhart, approved rate increases averaging 29 percent for Wellmark Blue Cross and Blue Shield, the state's dominant health insurer, and 20 percent for Coventry Health Care....

... in Hawaii, the insurance commissioner this month approved rate increases averaging 27 percent for the Hawaii Medical Service Association and 34 percent for Kaiser Permanente health plans.

338) **After Obamacare caused Obama supporting graduate students at the University of Missouri to lose their insurance, they falsely blamed it on the school**

In August 2015, the University of Missouri issued the following message to its graduate students:

"The Affordable Care Act prevents employers from giving employees money specifically so they can buy health insurance on the individual market. Graduate teaching and research assistants are classified as employees by the IRS, so they fall under this ruling."

However, in November 2015, left wing graduate students who had voted for Obama, falsely blamed their loss of insurance on the school, instead of on Obamacare.

339) **A federal judge ruled that some of the funding for Obamacare was unconstitutional**

In May 2016, U.S. District Court Judge Rosemary Collyer ruled that some of the funding for Obamacare was unconstitutional, because it had not been approved by Congress.

340) Obama falsely said that opponents of Obamacare did not have a plan to replace it

In November 2016, when talking about Republican opponents of Obamacare, Obama said:

"You watch the press conference and you realize, they got no plan... It's not like, they don't even have a pretense of a plan. They don't even have a semblance of a plan. Not even a hint of a plan. Not even a remote — not even a — there's no plan. Nothing, zero, nada. You can't just be against something. You gotta be for something."

However, several months earlier, in June 2016, the Republicans had announced this plan to replace Obamacare.

341) Obama falsely said that none of the predictions that were made by Obamacare opponents came true

In November 2016, when talking about predictions made by Obamacare opponents, Obama said:

"None of what they said has happened."

However, in the real world, Obamacare opponents accurately predicted that Obamacare would cause millions of people to lose their insurance.

* * * * * * END OF BOOK * * * * * * *